A

CATALOGUE OF LAW BOOKS,

PUBLISHED AND FOR SALE

BY

CHARLES C. LITTLE AND JAMES BROWN.

THE LAWBOOK EXCHANGE, LTD.
Clark, New Jersey
2007

ISBN-13: 978-1-58477-825-7
ISBN-10: 1-58477-825-3

The quality of this reprint is equivalent to the quality of the original work.

THE LAWBOOK EXCHANGE, LTD.
33 Terminal Avenue
Clark, New Jersey 07066-1321

Please see our website for a selection of our other publications and fine facsimile reprints of classic works of legal history:
www.lawbookexchange.com

Library of Congress Cataloging-in-Publication Data

A catalogue of law books, published and for sale by Charles C. Little and James Brown.
p. cm.
Originally published: A catalogue of law books, published and for sale by Charles C. Little and James Brown. Boston : Printed by Freeman and Bolles : [Little and Brown], 1846.
Includes index.
ISBN-13: 978-1-58477-825-7 (cloth : alk. paper)
ISBN-10: 1-58477-825-3 (cloth : alk. paper)
1. Law--Bibliography--Catalogs. 2. Law--United States--Bibliography. I. Charles C. Little and James Brown (Firm)
KF6.C38 2007
016.34--dc22 2007000118

Printed in the United States of America on acid-free paper

A

CATALOGUE OF LAW BOOKS

PUBLISHED AND FOR SALE

BY

CHARLES C. LITTLE AND JAMES BROWN.

COLLEGE BUILDINGS,
NO. 112, WASHINGTON STREET.

BOSTON:

PRINTED BY FREEMAN AND BOLLES.

MDCCCXLVI.

A

CATALOGUE OF LAW BOOKS,

PUBLISHED AND FOR SALE

BY

CHARLES C. LITTLE AND JAMES BROWN.

BOSTON:
1846.

ADVERTISEMENT.

SINCE the publication of our last Law Catalogue, in 1844, we have received large accessions to our stock from the principal European markets, and the contributions of the American press. We beg leave to call the attention of the Profession, especially to the valuable works on the Civil Law — the large list of French Law Books — the very complete collection of early and late English Reports and Elementary works; and, in American Books, to our own editions of VESEY, JR. by SUMNER — the UNITED STATES DIGEST, by METCALF, PERKINS and CURTIS, being a complete Digest of more than 600 volumes of Reports, now completed — the EDITION OF THE LAWS OF THE UNITED STATES, in seven super-royal 8vo volumes, published by order and under the patronage of Government — GREENLEAF ON EVIDENCE, 2 volumes — MR. JUSTICE STORY'S COMPLETE WORKS, &c. &c.

To the present Catalogue we have added an alphabetical Index to all the Reports, with the abbreviations, and a corrected copy of Prof. Greenleaf's "Catalogue of a Select Law Library," which the author has been kind enough to revise for the purpose.

A new Catalogue of our Miscellaneous Stock, including a large collection, many of them rare and of great value, made during the past season by one of our House from the principal European markets, will be published in the course of next month, and may be had gratis, on application.

Orders for Books from England, France, and Germany are forwarded regularly by the steamers to competent and faithful agents in London, Paris and Leipsic.

It will be borne in mind, that the prices given in this Catalogue, are the usual retail prices, from which discounts are made varying with the amounts purchased at one time, and depending on the works selected.

112, Washington Street, April 18, 1846.

CONTENTS.

AMERICAN REPORTS.

United States.

1. Supreme Court.

Dallas's Reports. From August term, 1790, to August term, 1800. 4 vols.

Cranch's Reports. From 1800 to February term, 1815. 9 vols.

Wheaton's Reports. From February term, 1816, to January term, 1827, inclusive. 12 vols.

Peters's Reports. From 1827 to 1843. 17 vols.

Peters's Condensed Reports of Cases in the Supreme Court of the United States. 6 vols.

Howard's Reports. From 1843 to 1845. 3 vols.

2. Circuit Courts.

First Circuit.

Gallison's Reports. From 1812 to 1815, inclusive. 2 vols.

Mason's Reports. From 1816 to 1830, inclusive. 5 vols.

Sumner's Reports. From 1830 to 1839. 3 vols.

Story's Reports. From 1839 to 1845. 2 vols.

Second Circuit.

Paine's Reports. From 1810 to 1826. 1 vol.

Third Circuit.

Dallas's Reports. [The 2d, 3d, and 4th volumes contain cases decided in this court, from April term, 1792, to October term, 1806, inclusive.]

WASHINGTON's C. C. Reports. From 1803 to 1827. 4 vols.

PETERS's C. C. Reports. From 1803 to 1818. 1 vol.

BALDWIN's Reports. From October term, 1829, to April term, 1833, inclusive. 1 vol.

WALLACE, J. B., Reports, include the cases of May sessions, 1801. 1 vol.

WALLACE, J. W., from 1842 to , (in preparation.)

Fourth Circuit.

MARSHALL's Decisions, by Brockenbrough. From 1802 to 1832. 2 vols.

Seventh Circuit.

McLEAN's Reports. From 1829 to 1842. 2 vols.

3. DISTRICT COURTS.

District of Maine.

WARE's Reports. From 1822 to 1839. 1 vol.

District of New York.

VAN NESS's Prize Cases. 1814. 1 vol.

District of Pennsylvania.

PETERS's Admiralty Decisions. From 1792 to 1807. 2 vols.

Eastern District of Pennsylvania.

GILPIN's Reports. From November term, 1828, to February term, 1836, inclusive. 1 vol.

District of South Carolina.

BEE's Admiralty Reports. From 1792 to 1805. 1 vol.

OPINIONS.

GILPIN's Opinions of Attorneys General of the United States. 2 vols.

State Reports.

Maine.

GREENLEAF'S Reports. From 1820 to 1832. 9 vols.
FAIRFIELD'S Reports. From 1833 to 1835. 3 vols.
SHEPLEY'S Reports. From April term, 1836, to June term, 1841. 6 vols.
APPLETON'S Reports. From 1841 to 1843. 2 vols.
SHEPLEY'S Reports. from 1843 to the present time. 2 vols.

New Hampshire.

NEW HAMPSHIRE Reports. From 1816 to 1844. 11 vols.
ADAMS'S Reports. 1 vol. Being volume 1st of New Hampshire Reports.
RICHARDSON & WOODBURY'S Reports. 1 vol. Being volume 2d of New Hampshire Reports.

Vermont.

N. CHIPMAN'S Reports. From 1789 to 1791. 1 vol.
TYLER'S Reports. From 1801 to 1803. 2 vols.
BRAYTON'S Reports. From 1815 to 1819. 1 vol.
D. CHIPMAN'S Reports. From 1789 to 1825. 2 vols.
AIKEN'S Reports. For 1826 and 1827. 2 vols.
VERMONT Reports. From 1826 to 1837. 9 vols.
SHAW'S Reports. From 1837 to 1839. 2 vols.
WESTON'S Reports. From 1839 to 1842. 3 vols.
SLADE'S Reports. 1843. 1 vol.
WASHBURN'S Reports. 1844. 1 vol.

Massachusetts.

MASSACHUSETTS Reports. From 1804 to 1822. 17 vols.
PICKERING'S Reports. From 1822 to 1840. 24 vols.
METCALF'S Reports. From 1840 to 1845. 7 vols.
THACHER'S Criminal Reports, by WOODMAN.

Connecticut.

KIRBY'S Reports. From 1785 to 1788. 1 vol.
ROOT'S Reports. From 1789 to 1798. 2 vols.

Day's Reports. From 1802 to 1810. 5 vols.
Connecticut Reports. By Thomas Day. From June, 1814, to the present time. 16 vols.

New York.

Coleman's Cases. From 1794 to 1800. 1 vol.
Coleman & Caines's Cases. From 1794 to 1805. 1 vol.
Caines's Reports. From 1803 to 1805. 3 vols.
Caines's Cases. For 1804 and 1805. 2 vols.
Johnson's Cases. 1799 to 1803. 3 vols.
Johnson's Reports. From 1806 to 1823. 20 vols.
Johnson's Chancery Reports. From 1814 to 1823. 7 vols.
Cowen's Reports. From 1823 to 1828. 9 vols.
Wendell's Reports. From 1828 to 1841. 26 vols.
Hoffman's Reports. From 1839 to 1840. 1 vol.
Hill's Reports. From 1841 to 1845. 6 vols.
Whittlesey's Chancery Reports. From to , 1 vol.
Hopkins's Chancery Reports. From 1823 to 1826. 1 vol.
Paige's Chancery Reports. From 1828 to 1845. 10 vols.
Yeates's Select Cases. Published in 1811. 1 vol.
Anthon's Nisi Prius Cases. From 1808 to 1818. 1 vol.
Rogers's New York City Hall Recorder. From 1816 to 1821. 6 vols.
Wheeler's Criminal Cases. 3 vols.
Hall's Reports for the years 1828 and 1829. 2 vols.
Edwards's Chancery Reports. From 1831 to 1842. 3 vols.
Clarke's Chancery Reports. 1839 to 1841. 1 vol.

New Jersey.

Coxe's Reports. From 1790 to 1795. 1 vol.
Pennington's Reports. From 1806 to 1813. 2 vols.
Southard's Reports. From 1816 to 1820. 2 vols.
Halstead's Reports. From 1821 to 1831. 7 vols.
Green's Reports. From 1831 to 1836. 3 vols.
Green's Chancery Reports. From 1838 to 1841. 1 vol.
Harrison's Reports. From 1837 to 1843. 4 vols.
Spencer's Reports. 1842 to 1845. 1 vol.
Saxton's Chancery Reports. From 1830 to 1832. 1 vol.

Pennsylvania.

DALLAS's Reports. From 1754 to 1806. 4 vols.
ADDISON's Reports. From 1791 to 1799. 1 vol.
YEATES's Reports. From 1791 to 1808. 4 vols.
BINNEY's Reports. From 1799 to 1814. 6 vols.
SERGEANT and RAWLE's Reports. From 1818 to 1829. 17 vols.
RAWLE's Reports. From 1828 to 1835. 5 vols.
WHARTON's Reports. From 1835 to 1841. 6 vols.
PENNSYLVANIA Reports. From 1829 to 1832. 3 vols.
RAWLE, PENROSE, and WATTS. 2 vols. Being 1 and 2 of Pennsylvania Reports.
PENROSE and WATTS. 1, being vol. 3 of Pennsylvania Reports.
WATTS's Reports. From 1832 to 1840. 10 vols.
BROWNE's Reports. From 1806 to 1814. 2 vols.
MILES's Reports. From 1835 to 1840. 2 vols.
ASHMEAD's Reports. From 1808 to 1841. 2 vols.
WATTS and SERGEANT's Reports. From 1841 to 1844. 7 vols.
PENNSYLVANIA Law Journal. 1842 to 1845. 4 vols.

Delaware.

HARRINGTON's Reports. From 1832 to 1844. 3 vols.

Maryland.

HARRIS and MCHENRY's Reports. From 1700 to 1799. 4 vols.
HARRIS and JOHNSON. From 1800 to 1826. 7 vols.
HARRIS and GILL. From 1826 to 1829. 2 vols.
GILL and JOHNSON. From 1829 to 1840. 11 vols.
BLAND's Chancery Reports. From 1811 to 1841. 3 vols.

Virginia.

WYTHE's Chancery Reports. From 1790 to 1795. 1 vol.
WASHINGTON's Reports. From 1790 to 1796. 2 vols.
CALL's Reports. From 1790 to 1818. 6 vols.
HENNING and MUNFORD's Reports. From 1806 to 1809. 4 vols.
MUNFORD's Reports. From 1810 to 1820. 6 vols.

GILMER'S Reports. During 1820 and 1821. 1 vol.
RANDOLPH'S Reports. From 1821 to 1828. 6 vols.
LEIGH'S Reports. From 1829 to 1841. 11 vols.
JEFFERSON'S Reports. From 1730 to 1772. 1 vol.
VIRGINIA Cases. From 1789 to 1826. 2 vols.
ROBINSON'S Reports. 1842 to 1844. 2 vols.
GRATTAN'S Reports. From 1844. 1 vol.

North Carolina.

MARTIN'S Reports. 1 vol.
HAYWOOD'S Reports. From 1789 to 1806. 2 vols.
TAYLOR'S Reports. From 1799 to 1802. 1 vol.
TAYLOR'S Reports. From 1816 to 1818. 1 vol.
CONFERENCE Reports. By Cameron and Norwood. From 1800 to 1804. 1 vol.
MURPHEY'S Reports. From 1804 to 1819. 3 vols.
CAROLINA Law Repository. From 1813 to 1816. 2 vols.
HAWKS'S Reports. From 1820 to 1826. 4 vols.
RUFFIN'S Reports. (Bound with 1st volume of Hawks.)
DEVEREUX'S Reports. From 1826 to 1834. 4 vols.
DEVEREUX'S Equity Reports. From 1826 to 1834. 2 vols.
DEVEREUX and BATTLE'S Reports. From 1834 to 1840. 4 vols. 3d and 4th volumes bound in one.
DEVEREUX and BATTLE'S Equity Reports. From 1834 to 1840. 3 vols.
IREDELL'S Law Reports. From 1840 to 1845. 5 vols.
IREDELL'S Equity Reports. From 1840 to 1843. 2 vols.

South Carolina.

BAY'S Reports. From 1783 to 1804. 2 vols.
BREVARD'S Reports. From 1793 to 1816. 3 vols.
DESSAUSSURE'S Equity Reports. From the Revolution to 1813. 4 vols.
SOUTH CAROLINA Reports. From 1812 to 1816. 2 vols.
CONSTITUTIONAL Court Reports. For the year 1817. 2 vols.
NOTT and MCCORD'S Reports. From 1817 to 1820. 2 vols.
CONSTITUTIONAL Reports. From 1812 to 1816. 2 vols.
CONSTITUTIONAL Reports, N. S. By Mills. For 1817 and 1818. 2 vols.
HARPER'S Reports. For 1823 and 1824. 1 vol.

Harper's Equity Reports. 1824. 1 vol.
McCord's Reports. From 1820 to 1828. 4 vols.
McCord's Chancery Reports. From 1825 to 1827. 2 vols.
Bailey's Reports. From 1828 to 1832. 2 vols.
Bailey's Equity Reports. 1830 to 1831. 1 vol.
Hill's Reports. From 1833 to 1837. 3 vols.
Hill's Chancery Reports. 1838. 2 vols.
Rice's Reports. From 1838 to 1839. 1 vol.
Rice's Chancery Reports. From 1838 to 1839. 1 vol.
Riley's Chancery Cases. From 1836 to 1837. 1 vol.
Riley's Law Cases. From 1836 to 1837. 1 vol.
Cheves's Reports. From 1839 to 1840. 1 vol.
McMullan's Cases at Law. From 1840 to 1842. 2 vols.
Dudley's Law and Equity.
Spear's Law Reports. 1842 to 1844. 2 vols.
Spear's Equity Reports. 1842 to 1844. 1 vol.
McMullan's Equity Cases. 1840 to 1842. 1 vol.

Georgia.

Charlton's (T. U. P.) Reports. Cases decided previous to 1810. 1 vol.
Charlton's (R. M.) Reports. From 1811 to 1837. 1 vol.
Dudley's Reports. From 1821 to 1833. 1 vol.
Georgia Decisions. to 1844. 1 vol.

Alabama.

Alabama Reports. By H. Miner. From 1820 to 1826. 1 vol.
Stewart's Reports. From 1827 to 1831. 3 vols.
Stewart and Porter's Reports. From 1831 to 1834. 5 vols.
Porter's Reports. From 1834 to 1839. 9 vols.
Alabama Reports. New Series. From 1840 to 1844. 5 vols.

Louisiana.

Martin's Reports. From 1809 to 1823. 12 vols.
Martin's Reports. N. S. From 1823 to 1830. 8 vols.
Louisiana Reports. From 1830 to 1841. 16 vols.
(The first five volumes of Louisiana Reports, are by Miller; the others by Curry.)
Robinson's Reports. 1841 to 1844. 4 vols.

Mississippi.

WALKER's Reports. From 1818 to 1832. 1 vol.
HOWARD's Reports. From 1834 to 1843. 7 vols.
SMEDES and MARSHALL's Reports. 1843 to 1844. 3 vols.
FREEMAN's Chancery Reports. 1839 to 1843. 1 vol.
SMEDES and MARSHALL's Chancery Reports. 1840 to 1845. 2 vols.

Tennessee.

OVERTON's Tennessee Reports. From 1791 to 1815. 2 vols.
COOKE's Reports. From 1811 to 1814. 1 vol.
HEYWOOD's Reports. From 1816 to 1818. 3 vols.
PECK's Reports. From 1822 to 1824. 1 vol.
MARTIN and YERGER's Reports. From 1825 to 1828. 1 vol.
YERGER's Reports. From 1832 to 1837. 10 vols.
MEIGS's Reports. From 1838 to 1839. 1 vol.
HUMPHREY's Reports. From 1839 to 1845. 5 vols.

Kentucky.

HUGHES's Reports. From 1785 to 1801. 1 vol.
KENTUCKY Decisions. From 1801 to 1805. 1 vol.
HARDIN's Reports. From 1805 to 1808. 1 vol.
BIBB's Reports. From 1808 to 1817. 4 vols.
MARSHALL's (A. K.) Reports. From 1817 to 1821. 3 vols.
LITTEL's Reports. From 1822 to 1824. 5 vols.
LITTEL's Select Cases. From 1795 to 1821. 1 vol.
MONROE's Reports. From 1824 to 1828. 7 vols.
MARSHALL's (J. J.) Reports. From 1829 to 1832. 7 vols.
DANA's Reports. From 1833 to 1840. 9 vols.
B. MUNROE's Reports. 1840 to 1844. 4 vols.

Ohio.

HAMMOND's Ohio Reports. From 1821 to 1843. 9 vols.
WRIGHT's Reports. From 1831 to 1834. 1 vol.
WILCOX's Reports. From 1840 to 1841. 1 vol.
STANTON's Reports. 1841 to 1843. 3 vols.
WILCOX's Condensed Ohio Reports. 1 vol.
GRISWOLD's Reports. (In press.)

Indiana.

Blackford's Reports. From May, 1817, to 1841, inclusive. 5 vols.

Illinois.

Breese's Reports. From 1819 to 1830. 1 vol.
Scammon's Reports. From 1832 to 1844. 4 vols.

Missouri.

Missouri Reports. From 1821 to the present time. 8 vols.

Arkansas.

Pike's Reports. From 1837 to 1844. 5 vols.
English's Reports. From 1844. Part 1.

Michigan.

Harrington's Reports. 1 vol.
Walker's Chancery Cases. 1842 to 1845. 1 vol.

Wisconsin.

Burritt's Reports. (In preparation.)

Iowa.

Bradford's Reports. (In preparation.)

THE REPORTERS,

ALPHABETICALLY ARRANGED.

A GENERAL ALPHABETICAL INDEX TO AMERICAN, ENGLISH, IRISH, SCOTCH, AND COLONIAL REPORTS.

Abbreviations.	*Reporters or Reports.*	*No. of Vols.*	*States or Courts.*
Abr. Ca. Eq.	Abridgment of Cases in Equity.	2	Ch.
Act.	Acton.	1	P. C.
Ada.	Adams.	1	N. H.
Add.	Addams.	2	Eccl.
A. or Addis.	Addison.	1	Pa.
A. & E.	Adolphus & Ellis.	12	Q. B.
A. & E. N. S.	Adolphus & Ellis. N. S.	5	Q. B.
Aik.	Aiken.	2	Vt.
Ala. by M.	Alabama Reports by Minor.	1	Ala.
Ala.	Alabama Reports. N. S.	5	Ala.
Alc.	Alcock.	1	R. C.
Al. & Nap.	Alcock & Napier.	1	K. B.
Al.	Aleyn.	1	U. B.
A. J.	American Jurist.	28	
Amb.	Ambler.	1	Ch.
And.	Anderson.	1	C. P.
Andr.	Andrews.	1	K. B.
Anst.	Anstruther.	3	Ex.
Anth. N. P. C.	Anthon N. P. C.	1	N. Y.
Ann.	Annaly.	1	K. B.
Appl.	Appleton. (Same as 19 and 20 Maine Reports.)	2	Me.
Arm. & Mac.	Armstrong & McCartney.	1	N. P.
Arn. & Hodg.	Arnold & Hodges.	1	Q. B. B. C.
Arn.	Arnold.	2	C. P.
Ash. Tab.	Ashe's Tables.	1	K. B. C. P.
Ash.	Ashmead.	2	Pa.
Atch.	Atcheson.	1	K. B.
Atk.	Atkyns.	3	Ch.
Bail.	Bailey.	2	S. C.
Bail.	Bailey, (Ch.)	1	S. C.

Abbreviations.	*Reporters or Reports.*	*No. of Vols.*	*States or Courts.*
Baldw.	Baldwin.	1	U. S. 3 C.
B. & B.	Ball & Beatty.	2	Ch.
Barn. C.	Barnadiston.	1	Ch.
Barn. K. B.	Barnadiston.	2	K. B.
Barn. Pr.	Barnes's Cases of Practice.	2	
B. & A.	Barnwall & Alderson.	5	K. B.
B. & C.	Barnwall & Creswell.	10	K. B.
B. & Ad.	Barnwall & Adolphus.	5	K. B.
Bar. & Aust.	Barron & Austin.	1	E. C
Bar. & Arn.	Barron & Arnold.	1	E C.
Batt.	Batty.	1	K. B.
	Bay.	2	S. C.
Beat.	Beatty temp. Hart.	1	Ch.
Beav.	Beavan.	6	R. C.
Bee's Adm. R.	Bee's Admiralty Reports.	1	District S. C.
	Bellewe.	1	K. B. C. P.
Bell's Ca.	Bell's Cases. (Scotch.)	2	C. S.
Benl.	Benloe.	1	C. P.
Ben. & Dal.	Benloe & Dallison.	1	C. P.
Bert.	Berton's Reports. (New Brunswick.)	1	
	Bibb.	4	Ky.
Bing.	Bingham.	10	C. P.
Bing. N. C.	Bingham's New Cases.	6	C. P.
Bin.	Binney.	6	Pa.
Black.	Blackford.	5	Ind.
Bla. H.	Blackstone, H.	2	C. P.
Bla. W.	Blackstone, Sir Wm.	2	K. B. C. P. & Ch.
Bla.	Bland, (Ch.)	3	Md.
Bli.	Bligh.	3	H. L.
Bli. N. S.	Bligh, N. S.	11	H. L.
Bos. & P.	Bosanquet & Puller.	5	C. P.
Bosw.	Boswell. (Scotch.)	1	C. S.
Bott, S. C.	Botts's Settlement Cases.	3	K. B.
Brad.	Bradford. (In preparation.)	1	Iowa.
Bray.	Brayton.	1	Vt.
Bree.	Breese.	1	Ill.
Brev.	Brevard.	3	S. C.
Bri. J.	Bridgman, Sir John.	1	C. P.
Bri. O.	Bridgman, Sir Orlando.	1	C. P.
Brock.	Brockenbrough's Reports of Marshall's Decisions.	2	U. S. 4 C
Va Ca.	Brockenbrough & Holmes's Cases.	1	Va. Cases.
Va. Ca.	Brockenbrough's Cases.	2	Va. Cases.
B. & B.	Broderip & Bingham.	3	C. P.
B. N. C.	Brooke's New Cases.	1	
Bro. P. C.	Brown.	8	H. L.
Bro. C.	Brown.	4	Ch.
Br.	Browne.	2	Pa.
Brow. & G.	Brownlow & Goldsborough.	1	C. P.
Bru.	Bruce. (Scotch.)	2	C. S.
Buch.	Buchanan. (Scotch.)	1	C. S.
	Buck.	1	B.
Bulst.	Bulstrode.	1	K. B.
Bunb.	Bunbury.	1	Ex.

Abbreviations.	*Reporters or Reports.*	*No. of Vols.*	*States or Courts.*
	Burrett. (In preparation.)	1	Wisconsin.
Burr. S. C.	Burrow's Settlement Cases.	1	K. B.
B. M.	Burrow, (tem. Mansfield.)	5	K. B.
Cai.	Caine.	3	N. Y.
C. C. E.	Caine's Cases in Error.	2	N. Y.
	Call.	6	Va.
Cal. S. C.	Caldecot's Settlement Cases.	1	
Cal.	Calthrop.	1	K. B.
Cam. Norw.	Cameron & Norwood's Conference Reports.	1	N. C.
Camp.	Campbell.	4	N. P.
Car. & P.	Carrington & Payne.	9	N. P.
Car. & M.	Carrington & Marshman.	1	N. P.
Car. & K.	Carrington & Kirwan.	1	N. P.
Car. & Ol.	Carrow & Oliver.	1	R. C.
Car. & Ol.	Carrow & Oliver's Railway Cases.	1	
Car. L. Rep.	Carolina Law Repository.	2	N. C.
Cart.	Carter.	1	C. P.
Carth.	Carthew.	1	K. B.
Car.	Cary.	1	Ch.
C. C.	Cases in Chancery. Temp. Car. II.	3	Ch.
Ca. T. T.	Cases temp. Talbot.	1	Ch.
C. O. L. & E.	Cases and Opinions of eminent Counsel in Law and Equity.	2	
Ca. Pr.	Cases of Practice.	1	K. B.
Charl. T. U. P.	Charlton, T. U. P.	1	Ga.
Charl. R. M.	Charlton, R. M.	1	Ga.
Chev.	Cheves.	1	S. C.
Chip. N.	Chipman, N.	1	Vt.
Chip. D.	Chipman, D.	2	Vt.
Chit. P. C.	Chitty's Points of Practice Cases.	2	B. C.
C. C. C.	Choice Cases in Chancery.	1	Ch.
Clark & Fin.	Clark & Finnelly.	10	H. L.
Clar.	Clark, Ch.	1	N. Y.
Clay.	Clayton.	1	Ass.
Cock. & R.	Cockburn & Rowe.	1	E. C.
Co. or Reports.	Coke.	6	K. B. C. P. Ex.
C. & A.	Cook & Alcock.	1	K. B.
C.	Cooke.	1	C. P.
Coo.	Cooke.	1	Tenn.
C. G.	Cooke, Geo.	2	C. P.
Col. Ca.	Coleman's Cases.	1	N Y.
Col. C. C.	Coleman & Cawes' Cases.	1	N. Y.
Col. P. C.	Colles.	1	H. L.
Coll.	Collyer.	1	V. C.
Comb.	Comberbach.	1	K. B.
	Common Law R. (Philad.)	43	
Comy.	Comyns.	2	K. B. C. P. &c.
Cond. Ch.	Condensed Chancery.	16	
Cond. Eccl.	Condensed Ecclesiastical.	7	
Cond. Exch.	Condensed Exchequer.	6	

Abbreviations.	*Reporters or Reports.*	*No. of Vols.*	*States or Courts.*
For.	Forrest. 1 Part.		Ex.
Forb.	Forbes. (Scotch.)	1	C. S.
Fort.	Fortescue.	1	K. B. C. P. Ex. & Ch.
Fos.	Foster.	1	K. B.
Fount.	Fountain Hall. (Scotch.)		C. S.
F. & S.	Fox & Smith.	1	K. B.
Fr. E. C.	Fraser's Election Cases.	2	E. C.
Free.	Freeman.	2	K. B. C. P. &c.
Free.	Freeman, (Ch.)	1	Miss.
Free. C. C.	Freeman's Chancery Cases		
Gal.	Gallison.	2	U. S. I. C.
G. & D.	Gale & Davison.	3	Q. B.
G.	Gale.	2	Ex.
Ga. Dec.	Georgia Decisions.	1	Ga.
Gib.	Gibson. (Scotch.)	1	C. S.
Gill & J.	Gill & Johnson.	11	Md.
Gilb.	Gilbert.	1	Eq. Ex.
Gilb. Ca.	Gilbert's Cases in Law and Equity.	1	
Gil.	Gilmer.	1	Va.
Gil.	Gilmour. (Scotch.)	1	C. S.
Gilp.	Gilpin.	1	East. Dist. of Penn.
Gilp. Opin.	Gilpin's Opinions of Attorneys General, U. S.	2	
Glanv.	Glanville.	1	E. C.
Glasc.	Glascott's Reports.		
G. & J.	Glyn & Jameson.	2	B.
Godb.	Godbolt.	1	All the courts of Bench.
Gold.	Goldsborough.	1	All the Courts.
Gosf.	Gosford.		C. S.
Gow, N. P. C.	Gow's Nisi Prius Cases.	1	N. P.
Gowl. Pr.	Gowland's Points of Practice Cases.		
Gratt.	Grattan.	1	Va.
Greenl.	Greenleaf.	9	Me.
	Green.	3	N. J.
Griff. L. R.	Griffith's Law Register.	2	
	Griswold. (In press.)	1	Ohio.
Gwil.	Gwillim's Tithe Cases.		
Hagg.	Haggard.	3	Ad.
Hagg. Eccl.	Haggard.	4	Eccl.
Hail.	Hailes. (Scotch)		C. S.
	Hall.	2	N. Y.
Hall, L. J.	Hall's Law Journal.		
Hals.	Halstead.	7	N. J.
Ham.	Hammond.	9	Ohio.
Hanm.	Hanmer's R. of Ld. Kenyon	2	K. B.
Harc. Dec.	Harcarse's Decisions. (Scotch.)		C. S.
Hard.	Hardin.	1	Ky.
Hard.	Hardres.	1	U. B.
	Hare.	3	V. C.
Harg. St. Tr.	Hargrave, F. State Trials.	11	K. B.
Harring.	Harrington.	3	Del.

Abbreviations.	*Reporters or Reports.*	*No. of Vols.*	*States or Courts.*
Monr. B.	Monroe, B.	4	Ky.
Mor. Dic.	Morison's Dictionary of Court of Session Decisions. (Scotch.)	41	
Mos.	Mosely.	1	Ch.
Mo. & M.	Moody & Malkin.	2	N. P.
Mo. & R.	Moody & Robinson.	2	N. P.
Mo. C. C. R.	Moody's Crown Cases Reserved.	2	C. C.
	Moore.	1	K. B. C. P. Ex.
Mo. A.	Moore, A.	1	C. P.
Mo.	Moore.	12	C. P.
Mo. & P.	Moore & Payne.	5	C. P.
Mo. & S.	Moore & Scott.	4	C. P.
Mo. E. T.	Moore, E. T.	3	P. C.
	Moore, E. T., East India Appeals.	2	P. C.
Munf.	Munford.	6	Va.
Mur.	Murphey.	3	N. C.
Mur. & H.	Murphy & Hurlstone.	1	Ex.
Mur.	Murray. (Scotch.)	4	Jury Court.
Mylne & C.	Mylne & Craig.	4	Ch.
Mylne & K.	Mylne & Keen.	3	Ch.
Nel.	Nelson.	1	Ch.
Nev. & M.	Neville & Manning.	6	Q. B.
Nev. & P.	Neville & Perry.	3	Q. B.
N. & M.	Neville & Manning.	3	M. C.
N. & P.	Neville & Perry.	1	M. C.
New Benl.	New Benloe.	1	K. B. C. P. Ex.
N. H.	New Hampshire Reports, including Adams, Richardson & Woodbury.	11	
	New Reports. (See Bosanquet & Puller.)		
N. Y. T.	New York Term Rep. (See Caines.)		
Nic. Har. & Car.	Nicholl, Hare, & Carrow.	2	R. C.
Nol.	Nolan.	1	M. C.
N. C L. Rep.	North Carolina Law Repository.	2	
N. C. T.	North Carolina Term R. (See Taylor.)		
	Northington's Reports. (See Eden.)		
N. & Mc.	Nott & McCord.	2	S. C.
	Noy.	1	K. B. C. P.
Over.	Overton.	2	Tenn.
	Owen.	1	K. B. C. P.
	Paige. Ch. R.	10	N. Y.
	Paine.	1	U. S. 2d C.
Pal.	Palmer.	1	K. B. C. P.
Park.	Parker.	1	Ex.
Peake, N. P. C.	Peake's Nisi Prius Cases.	2	N. P.

TABLE

SHOWING THE CONTENTS OF THE CONDENSED REPORTS IN THIS CATALOGUE.

Condensed Chancery Reports, by Richard Peters and E. D. Ingraham.

Vol. 1. Simons and Stuart, vols. 1 and 2.
Vol. 2. Simons, vols. 1 and 2.
Vol. 3. Russell, vols. 1, 2, 3, 4.
Vol. 4. Russell and Mylne, vol. 1.
Vol. 5. Simons, vol. 3; Tamlyn, vol. 1.
Vol. 6. Simons, vols. 4, 5; Russell and Mylne, vol. 2; Mylne and Keen, vol. 1.
Vol. 7. Mylne and Keen, vols. 1, 2; Simons, vol. 5.
Vol. 8. Mylne and Keen, vols. 2 and 3; Cooper's Select Cases, vol. 1.
Vol. 9. Mylne and Keen, vol. 3; Simons, vols. 6, 7.
Vol. 10. Simons, vol. 7; Mylne and Keen, vol. 3; Lloyd and Goold, vol. 1.
Vol. 11. Turner and Russell, vol. 1; Simons, vol. 8.
Vol. 12. Molloy, vols. 1 and 2.
Vol. 13. Russell and Mylne, vol. 2; Mylne and Craig, vol. 1.
Vol. 14. Mylne and Craig, vols. 2 and 3.
Vol. 15. Keene, vols. 1 and 2.
Vol. 16. Simons, vols. 9 and 10.

English Common Law Reports, Edited by Sargeant and Lowber.

Vol. 1. Taunton, vols. 5 and 6.
Vol. 2. Taunton, vol. 7; Starkie, vol. 1.
Vol. 3. Holt, vol. 1; Starkie, vol. 2.
Vol. 4. Taunton, vol. 8; Marshall, 2 vols.; Moore, 3 vols.
Vol. 5. Broderip and Bingham, vol. 1; Barnewall and Alderson, vol. 3; Gow, vol. 1, pt. 1.
Vol. 6. Broderip and Bingham, vol. 2; Barnewall and Alderson, vol. 4.
Vol. 7. Barnewall and Alderson, vol. 5; Broderip and Bingham, vol. 8.
Vol. 8. Barnewall and Creswell, vol 1; Bingham, vol. 2.
Vol. 9. Barnewall and Creswell, vol. 2; Bingham, vol. 2.
Vol. 10. Barnewall and Creswell, vols. 3, 4.
Vol. 11. Bingham, vol. 3; Barnewall and Creswell, vol. 5; Carr. and Payne, vol. 1.
Vol. 12. Carr. and Payne, vol. 2; Barnewall and Creswell, vol. 5.
Vol. 13. Bingham, vols. 3, 4; Barnewall and Creswell, vol. 6.
Vol. 14. Barnewall and Creswell, vol. 7; Starkie, vol. 3; Carr. and Payne, vol. 3.
Vol. 15. Bingham, vols. 4, 5; Barnewall and Creswell, vol. 8.
Vol. 16. Dowling and Ryland, vol. 8; Moor, vols. 4 and 5.
Vol. 17. Moore, vols. 6, 7, 8, 9, 10; Moore and Payne, 1, 2; Manning and Ryland, vols. 1, 2; Barnewall and Creswell, vol. 9.
Vol 18. Chitty, 2 vols.
Vol. 19. Bingham, vol. 6; Carr. and Payne, vol. 4.
Vol. 20. Bingham, vol. 7; Barnewall and Adolphus, vol. 1.
Vol. 21. Barnewall and Creswell, vol. 10; Bingham, vol. 8; Ryan and Moody.
Vol. 22. Barnewall and Adolphus, vol. 2; Moody and Malkin, vol. 1; Dowling and Ryland, vol. 9; Moore, vols. 11 and 12.
Vol. 23. Barnewall and Adolphus, vol. 3; Bingham, vol. 9.
Vol. 24. Barnewall and Adolphus, vol. 4; Carr. and Payne, vol. 6.
Vol. 25. Bingham, vol. 10; Carr. and Payne, vol. 6.
Vol. 26. Douglass, 3, 4.
Vol. 27. Barnewall and Adolphus, vol. 5; Bingham's New Cases, vol. 1.

Vol. 28. Adolphus and Ellis, vol. 1; Moore and Scott, vols. 1, 2; Neville and Manning, vols. 1, 2, 3.
Vol. 29. Adolphus and Ellis, vol. 2; Bingham's New Cases, vol. 2.
Vol. 30. Adolphus and Ellis, vol. 3; Moore and Scott, vols. 3 and 4; Neville and Manning, vol. 4; Scott, vol. 2.
Vol. 31. Adolphus and Ellis, vols. 4 and 5.
Vol. 32. Bingham's New Cases, vol. 3; Carrington and Payne, vol. 7.
Vol. 33. Adolphus and Ellis, vol. 6; Bingham's New Cases, vol. 4.
Vol. 34. Adolphus and Ellis, vol. 7; Carrington and Payne, vol. 8.
Vol. 35. Bingham, vol. 5; Adolphus and Ellis, vol. 8.
Vol. 36. Adolphus and Ellis, vol. 9: Scott, vols. 3 and 4: Neville and Manning, vols. 5 and 6; Neville and Perry, vol. 1.
Vol. 37. Adolphus and Ellis, vol. 10: Bingham's New Cases, vol. 6.
Vol. 38. Carrington and Payne, vol. 9: Deacon's Bankruptcy, vol. 1.
Vol. 39. Adolphus and Ellis, vol. 11: Manning and Granger, vol. 1.
Vol. 40. Adolphus and Ellis, vol. 12: Manning and Granger, vol. 2.
Vol. 41. Adolphus and Ellis, N. S. vol. 1, and Carrington and Marshman, vol. 1.
Vol. 42. Adolphus and Ellis, N. S. vol. 2, and Manning and Granger, vol. 3.
Vol. 43. Adolphus and Ellis, N. S. vol. 3, and Manning and Granger, vol. 5.
Vol. 44. Manning and Granger, vol. 4.

N. B. — A General Index of the above series of Reports is in preparation. Since vol. 40, the English Reports have been reprinted in full.

RESERVED CROWN CASES, EDITED BY J. W. WALLACE.

Vol. 1. Russell and Ryan's Crown Cases.
Vol 2. Moody's Crown Cases.
Vol. 3. Jebb's Crown Cases.

ENGLISH EXCHEQUER REPORTS, CONDENSED AND EDITED BY F. J. TROUBAT, ESQ.

Vol. 1. Price's Reports, 3 vols.
Vol. 2. Price's Reports, vols. 4, 5, 6.
Vol. 3. Price's Reports, vols. 7, 8.
Vol. 4. Price's Reports, vols. 9, 10: Daniell, vol. 1.
Vol. 5. Price's Reports, vols. 11, 12.
Vol. 6. Price's Reports, vol. 10, pt. 3d, vol. 13, McCleland, Wightwick.

N. B. — Since vol. 6 of the above, the English Exchequer Reports are reprinted in full.

ENGLISH ECCLESIASTICAL REPORTS, EDITED BY E. D. INGRAHAM, ESQ.

Vol. 1. Phillimore's Reports, 3 vols.
Vol. 2. Addams's Reports, 3 vols.
Vol. 3. Haggard's Reports, vol. 1, Fergusson.
Vol. 4. Haggard's Reports, vol. 2: Haggard's Consistory Reports, 2 vols.
Vol. 5. Haggard's Reports, vol. 3: Lee's Reports, vol. 1.
Vol. 6. Curteis's Reports, vol. 1: Lee's Reports, vol. 2.
Vol. 7. Curteis's Reports, vols. 2 and 3.

CONDENSED REPORTS OF THE SUPREME COURT OF THE UNITED STATES. R. D. PETERS, EDITOR.

Vol. 1. Dallas's Reports, vols. 2, 3, 4: Cranch's Reports, vols. 1, 2, 3.
Vol. 2. Cranch, vols. 4, 5, 6, 7.
Vol. 3. Cranch's Reports, vols. 8, 9; Wheaton, vol. 1.
Vol. 4. Wheaton's Reports, vols. 2, 3, 4, 5.
Vol. 5. Wheaton's Reports, vols. 6, 7, 8, 9.
Vol. 6. Wheaton's Reports, vols. 10, 11, 12.

CATALOGUE

OF

A Select Law Library.

It is supposed that every member of the profession will furnish himself with the Statutes, Digests, and Reports of his own State, and with the Elementary Treatises on its peculiar jurisprudence. This catalogue, therefore, principally embraces the Books which are useful to every American Lawyer, in whatever State he may reside. Those deemed the most essential in each class are marked thus (*).

Class I. includes those which are most useful and important for persons of limited means.

Class II. includes those which are highly useful, but not indispensable, and are auxiliary to the former.

ABRIDGMENTS.

Class I.

Bacon's Abridgment, by Bouvier.
*Bouvier's Law Dictionary.
*Comyn's Digest.
Jacob's Law Dictionary, by Tomlins.

Class II.

Dane's Abridgment.
Petersdorff's Abridgment.
Rolle's Abridgment.
*Viner's Abridgment, and Supplement.

GENERAL TREATISES.

*Blackstone's Commentaries.
*Kent's Commentaries.
Crabbe's History of English Law.

CLASS I.

Story, on the Conflict of Laws.

CLASS II.

Hale's History of the Common Law.
*Hoffman's Course of Legal Study.
Hoffman's Legal Outlines.
Reeves's History of English Law.
Wilson's Law Lectures.
*Wooddeson's Lectures.

INDEXES AND DIGESTS.

American Digest, by Anthon and others.
*American Chancery Digest, by Wheeler.
*Chitty's Digest of Equity Cases.
Coventry and Hughes's Index to the old Common Law Reports.
*Curtis's Digest of Admiralty Decisions.
*Harrison's Digest of Modern Common Law Reports.
United States Digest.
*Peters's Digest Supreme Court Reports.
Wheaton's Digest of Supreme Court Reports.
Washburn's Digest of Vermont Reports.
*Benjamin and Sliddel's enlarged Digest of Louisiana Reports.
Minot's Digest of Massachusetts Reports.
Bridgman's Digest of Equity Reports.
Campbell and Cambreleng's Equity Digest.
*Clerke's Digest New York Reports.
*Coxe's Digest of Supreme Court Reports.
Dorsey's Digest Alabama Reports.
Gilman's Digest Indiana and Illinois Reports.
Wilcox's Digest Ohio Reports.
Dutton's Connecticut Digest.
Greenleaf's Digest of Maine Reports.
Halstead's Digest New Jersey Reports.
Hall's Digest Virginia Reports.
Irepell's Digest North Carolina Reports.
Johnson's Digest of New York Reports.
Maddy's Digest of Ecclesiastical Reports.
Manning's Index to Nisi Prius Reports.

Class I.

Class II.

Munford's Index to Virginia Authorities.
Rice's Digest South Carolina Reports.
*Tomlin's Index to Criminal Law.
Tomlin's Repertorium Juridicum.
Wharton's Digest of Pennsylvania Reports.
Wharton's Digest of Southern and Western Reports.

ELEMENTARY TREATISES.

I. On Real Property.

*Angell on Watercourses.
Burton's Compendium of Real Property.
*Coke on Littleton, by Butler.
*Cruise's Digest.
*Fearne on Remainders, by Butler.
Flintoff on Real Property.
*Jarman on Wills, by Perkins.
*Powell on Devises, by Jarman.
*——— on Mortgages, by Coventry and Rand.
Preston on Estates.
*Sanders on Uses and Trusts.
*Sheppard's Touchstone.
Sugden on Powers.
*——— on Vendors.
Watkins on Conveyancing.
*Wigram on Interpretation of Wills.

Angell on Adverse Enjoyment.
Bacon on Uses.
Barton's Elements of Conveyancing.
*Chance on Powers.
*Chitty on Descents.
Coke on Littleton, by Thomas.
Coote on Mortgages.
Haye's on Limitations in Devises.
Lomax's Digest.
Park on Dower.
Powell on Powers.
Roberts on Fraudulent Conveyances.
Sullivan's Law Lectures.
Watkins on Descents, by Williams.
*Woodfall on Landlord and Tenant.
Wright on Tenures.

II. On Persons and Personal Property.

Amos on Fixtures.
*Angell and Ames on Corporations.
Atherly on Marriage Settlements.

Bingham on Judgments.
Bradby on Distresses.
Chitty on Prerogative.
*Clancy on Rights of Married Women.

CLASS I.

*Bingham on Infancy.
Caldwell on Arbitrations.
*Chitty on Contracts.
Macpherson on Infancy.
Pitman on Principal and Surety.
Platt on Covenants.
*Roberts on Frauds.
*——— on Fraudulent Conveyances.
*Roper on Husband and Wife.
*——— on Legacies, by White.
Shelford on Lunatics.
*Story on Bailments.
Story on Contracts.
*Watson on Arbitrations.
*Webster on Patents.
*Williams on Executors and Administrators.

CLASS II.

Collinson on Idiots and Lunatics.
*Comyn on Contracts.
Ellis on the Law of Debtor and Creditor.
Godson on Patents.
*Hargrave's Law Tracts.
*Hovenden on Frauds.
Jones on Carriers.
Jones on Bailments.
*Kyd on Awards.
——— on Corporations.
*Phillips on Patent Rights.
Pothier on Obligations, by Evans.
Powell on Contracts.
Reeve's Domestic Relations.
Toller on Executors and Administrators.
Woolrych on Window Lights.

III. COMMERCIAL AND MARITIME LAW.

*Abbott on Shipping, by Story, (1829.)
Bayley on Bills of Exchange, and Promissory Notes, by Phillips and Sewall, (1836.)
*Collyer on Partnership.
Long on Sales, by Rand.
*Phillips on Insurance.
Pitman on Principal and Surety.
Pothier on Maritime Contracts, by Cushing.
Stephens on Average, and Benecke on Insurance, by Phillips.
*Story on Agency.
*——— on Bills.
*——— on Partnership.
Theobald on Principal and Surety.
Chitty and Hulme on Bills.
*Story on Promissory Notes.
Bell's Commercial Law of Scotland.
*Brown's Civil and Admiralty Law.
Cary on Partnership.
Chitty on Bills.
*Chitty's Commercial Law.
Commercial Code of France, by Rodman.
Emerigon on Bottomry, by Hall.
*Fell on Guarantee.
*Gow on Partnership.
*Holt on Shipping.
Hughes on Insurance.
Jacobson's Sea Laws, by Frick.
Lawes on Charter Parties.
Livermore on Agency.
*Marshall on Insurance.
Molloy de Jure Martimo.
*Montague on Lien and Set-off.
*Paley on Agency, by Llyod.

Class I.

*Duer on Insurance.

Class II.

Park on Insurance.
Reeves on Shipping.
Roscoe on Bills of Exchange.
Watson on Partnership.
Weskett on Insurance.

IV. Pleadings and Actions.

*Adams on Ejectment, by Tillinghast.
*Angell on Limitations.
*Chitty on Pleading.
*Jackson on Real Actions.
Starkie on Criminal Pleadings.
——— on Slander.
*Stearns on Real Actions.
*Stephen on Pleading.

Booth on Real Actions.
Fitzherbert's Natura Brevium.
Archbold on Criminal Law and Pleadings.
Babington on Set-off.
Barbour on Set-off.
*Bradby on Distresses.
Chitty's Precedents.
Gilbert on Distresses.
*Gould on Pleading.
Hammond on Parties.
*Lawes on Assumpsit.
——— on Pleading.
Oliver's Precedents.
——— Forms.
*Roscoe on Real Actions.
Runnington on Ejectment.
Sanders on Pleading and Evidence.
Story on Pleading.
Wilkinson on Limitations.
——— on Replevin.

V. Law of Evidence.

*Beck's Medical Jurisprudence.
*Greenleaf on Evidence.
*Phillips on Evidence. 9th ed.
*Starkie on Evidence.

Gilbert on Evidence, by Loft.
*Best on Presumptions.
McNally on Evidence.
*Paris and Fonblanque on Medical Jurisprudence.
*Peake on Evidence, by Norris.
Pritchard on Insanity.
Ray on Insanity.
Roscoe on Evidence.
Roscoe's Criminal Evidence.
Swift on Evidence.

CLASS I.

CLASS II.

Van Heythuysen on Marine Evidence.
Wills on Circumstantial Evidence.

VI. PRACTICE AND NISI PRIUS PROCEEDINGS.

Clerke's Admiralty Practice, by Hall.
*Dunlap's Admiralty Practice.
Leigh's Nisi Prius.
Macqueen's Practice in the House of Lords.
Roscoe's Nisi Prius.
*Selwyn's Nisi Prius.
Stephens's Nisi Prius.
*Tidd's Practice.

*Buller's Nisi Prius.
*Chitty's Practice of the Law.
*Conklin's Practice.
*Graham on New Trials.
Graham's Practice, (in New York.)
Howe's Practice, (in Massachusetts.)
Manning's Exchequer Practice.
Modern Practice of the Exchequer, (1731.)
Paine and Duer's Practice, (in New York.)
Robinson's Practice, (in Virginia.)
Troubat and Haly's Practice, (in Pennsylvania.)

VII. ON EQUITY JURISPRUDENCE.

Drewry on Injunctions.
*Eden on Injunctions.
*Fonblanque on Equity.
*Story's Commentaries on Equity.

Boyle on Charities.
Duke on Charitable Uses, by Bridgman.
Jeremy on Equity.
*Maddock's Chancery Principles and Practice.
*Newland on Contracts in Equity.

VIII. ON EQUITY AND PRACTICE.

Barton's Suit in Equity.
Beames's Pleas in Equity.
Blake's Chancery Practice.
*Cooper on Equity Pleadings.
*Daniel's Chancery Practice.
*Farren's Common Forms for drawing Bills.

Beames's Ordinances in Chancery.
Bennet's Practice in the Master's office.
Gilbert's Forum Romanum.
Grant's Chancery Practice.
Hand's Solicitor in Chancery.

Class I.

*Hoffman's Chancery Practice.
*——— Master in Chancery.
*Mitford (Lord Redesdale) on Equity Pleadings.
Newland's Chancery Practice.
Seton's Forms of Decrees.
*Story's Equity Pleadings.
Welford's Pleadings in Equity.

Class II.

Hare on Discovery.
*Harrison's Chancery Practice.
Hinde's Chancery Practice.
Montague on Equity Pleadings.
*Paine and Duer's Practice.
Robinson's Practice.
*Smith's Chancery Practice.
Van Heythuysen's Equity Draftsman.
Wigram on Discovery.
Wyatt's Practical Register.

IX. Criminal Law.

Deacon's Criminal Law.
East's Pleas of the Crown.
*Russell on Crimes.

Archbold on Criminal Law.
Beccaria on Crimes.
Burns's Justice of the Peace.
*Chitty's Criminal Law.
Foster's Crown Law.
Gabbett's Criminal Law.
Hale's Pleas of the Crown.
*Hawkins's Pleas of the Crown, by Leach.
Holt on Libels.

X. Law of Nations and Prizes.

*Brown's Civil and Admiralty Law.
*Rutherforth's Institutes.
Story on the Conflict of Laws.
Vattel on Law of Nations.
*Wheaton on International Law.
——— on Captures.

*Bynkershoeck on War, by Duponceau.
Chitty on Captures.
*Grotius on the Law of Nations.
Lee on Captures.
Mackintosh on National Law.
*Martens on the Law of Nations.
——— on Privateers.
Puffendorf on the Law of Nations.
Reddie on International Law.
Ward on the Law of Nations.

CLASS I. | CLASS II.

XI. CIVIL AND FOREIGN LAW.

*Cooper's Justinian's Institutes.
*Domat on the Civil Law, by Strahan.
Erskine's Institutes of the Law of Scotland.
Irving's Introduction to the Civil Law.
*Pothier's Works, (Œuvres de Pothier.)
Pothier on Sales, by Cushing.
The Partidas, by Moreau and Carleton.
*Toullier on the Civil Code. (Toullier Droit Civil François.)
*Mackeldey's Roman Law, by Kaufmann.

*Ayliffe's Pandect.
Brown's Civil and Admiralty Law.
Civil Code of Louisiana.
Code of Procedure of Louisiana.
Corpus Juris Civilis Academicum.
*Halifax on Roman and Civil Law.
*Heineccii Elem. Juris. Civ. Secund. Ordin. Pand.
Stair's Institutions by Brodie.
The Digest and Code, (Pandectæ Justinianæ.)
Vicat's Vocabulary.
Vinnius ad Institut.
White's New Recopilacion.
Savigny's History of the Roman Law.
——— Treatise on the Roman Law.
Wood's Civil Law.
Grotius's Introduction to Dutch Jurisprudence, by Herbert.

ENGLISH REPORTS.

I. COMMON LAW.

*Adolphus and Ellis's Reports.
*Barnewall and Alderson's Reports.
*——— and Creswell's Reports.
*——— and Adolphus's Reports.
*Bingham's Reports.
*——— New Cases.
*Blackstone's (Henry) Reports.
——— (William) Reports, by Ellsley.
*Bosanquet and Puller's Reports.
*Broderip and Bingham's Reports.
*Burrow's Reports.

Aleyn's Reports.
Anderson's Reports.
Andrews's Reports.
*Bannister's Reports of Sir O. Bridgman.
Barnardiston's Reports in King's Bench.
Benloe and Dallison's Reports.
*Bligh's Reports in House of Lords. 1st Series. 2d Series.
*Brown's Parliamentary Reports, by Tomlins.
Brownlow and Goldsborough's Reports.

Class I.

Clark and Finelly's Reports.
*Coke's Reports.
*Cowper's Reports.
*Croke's Reports.
*Douglas's Reports.
Dow and Clark's Reports.
*Durnford and East's Reports.
*East's Reports.
Hobart's Reports, by Williams.
*Manning and Granger's Reports.
*Maule and Selwyn's Reports.
*Meeson and Welsby's Reports.
Plowden's Reports.
*Raymond's (Lord) Reports, by Bayley.
*Salkeld's Reports, by Evans.
*Saunders's Reports, by Williams.
*Strange's Reports, by Nolan.
*Taunton's Reports.
*Willes's Reports.
*Wilson's Reports.

Class II.

Bulstrode's Reports.
Bunbury's Reports.
Carter's Reports.
*Carthew's Reports.
*Cases tempore Hardwicke.
Comberbach's Reports.
*Comyns's Reports.
*Crompton and Jervis's Reports.
*——— and Meeson's Reports.
*——— Meeson and Roscoe's Reports.
*Dow's Parliamentary Reports.
Dyer's Reports, by Vaillant.
Fitzgibbon's Reports.
Forrests's Reports.
Fortescue's Reports.
*Freeman's Reports in King's Bench, by Smirke.
Godbolt's Reports.
Hardres's Reports.
Hetley's Reports.
Hutton's Reports.
*Jenkins's Reports.
Jones's (Sir William) Reports.
——— (Sir Thomas) Reports.
Keble's Reports.
Keilway's Reports.
Lane's Reports.
Latch's Reports.
*Leach's Reports.
*Leonard's Reports.
*Levinz's Reports, by Salkeld.
*Modern Reports.
*Moore's Reports.
Moore and Payne's Reports.
——— and Scott's Reports.
Owen's Reports.
Palmer's Reports.
Parker's Reports.
Pollexfen's Reports.
Popham's Reports.
Price's Reports.

CLASS I.

CLASS II.

Raymond's (Sir Thomas) Reports.
Ridgeway's Parliamentary Reports.
*Rolle's Reports.
*Russell and Ryan's Crown Cases.
*Ryan and Moody's Crown Cases.
Saville's Reports.
Sayer's Reports.
Scott's Reports.
*Shower's Reports.
Siderfin's Reports.
Skinner's Reports.
*Style's Reports.
*Tyrrwhitt's Reports.
Vaughan's Reports.
*Ventris's Reports.
Wightwick's Reports.
Winch's Reports.
Year Books.
*Yelverton's Reports, by Metcalf.

II. EQUITY REPORTS.

*Ambler's Reports, by Blunt.
*Atkyns's Reports, by Sanders.
*Brown's Chancery Reports, by Belt. New ed. by Perkins.
*Cooper's Equity Reports.
*Cox's Reports.
*Craig & Phillips's Reports.
*Eden's Reports.
*Equity Cases Abridged.
*Freeman's Reports, by Hovenden.
*Jacob and Walker's Reports.
*Jacob's Reports.
*Merivale's Reports.
*Mylne and Keen's Reports.
——— and Craig's Reports.
Peere Williams's Reports, by Cox.

*Anstruther's Reports.
*Ball and Beatty's Reports.
Barnardiston's Reports in Chancery.
Beavan's Reports.
Cary's Reports.
*Cases in Chancery.
Cases Tempore Talbot, by Forrester.
Daniel's Equity Reports.
Dickens's Reports.
Gilbert's Equity Reports.
Hanmer's Reports.
Hare's Reports.
Kelyng's (William) Equity Reports.
Maddock's Reports.
McClelland's Reports.

CLASS I.

*Phillips's Reports.
Precedents in Chancery.
*Russell's Reports.
*Russell and Mylne's Reports.
*Schoales & Lefroy's Reports.
*Swanston's Reports.
*Turner and Russell's Reports.
*Vernon's Reports, by Raithby.
*Vesey's (Senior) Reports, by Belt.
*——— (Junior) Reports, by Sumner.
*Vesey and Beames's Reports.
*Younge and Collyer's Reports.

CLASS II.

McClelland and Younge's Reports.
*Moseley's Reports.
Price's Reports.
Reports in Chancery.
Reports tempore Finch.
Select Cases in Chancery.
*Simons & Stuart's Reports.
*Simons's Reports.
*Tamlyn's Reports.
Tothill's Transactions, (or Reports.)
West's Reports.
Wilson's Reports.
Younge and Jervis's Reports.
Younge's Reports.

III. ADMIRALTY REPORTS.

*Dodson's Reports.
*Edwards's Reports.
*Haggard's Admiralty Reports.
*Robinson's Reports.
*——— New Reports.
Acton's Reports.
Marriott's Reports.
Stewart's Admiralty Reports.

IV. ECCLESIASTICAL REPORTS.

*Addams's Ecclesiastical Reports.
*Haggard's Consistory Reports.
*——— Ecclesiastical Reports.
Lee's Ecclesiastical Reports, by Phillimore.
Phillimore's Eccl. Reports.
Fergusson's Reports on Marriage and Divorce.

V. NISI PRIUS REPORTS.

*Campbell's Reports.
*Espinasse's Reports.
Moody and Malkin's Reports.
——— and Robinson's Reports.
Ryan and Moody's Reports.
*Starkie's Reports.
Carrington and Marshman's Reports.
——— and Payne's Reports.
Gow's Reports.
*Holt's Reports.
*Peake's Reports.

For AMERICAN REPORTS, see p. iv.

CATALOGUE OF LAW BOOKS.

ABBOTT (Charles, Ld. Tenterden.) Treatise of the Law relative to Merchant Ships and Seamen; 5th Am. from the 6th Lond. ed. by John Henry Abbott, with Annotations by Joseph Story, and an Appendix containing the American Acts respecting the Registry and Navigation of Ships. The whole edited from the new Edition of Mr. Sergeant Shee, by J. C. Perkins, Esq. Boston. 1846

ABBOTT (Joel.) Trial by General Naval Court Martial on Charges made by Com. Porter. 8vo. 1,00. Boston. 1822

ACHERLY (Roger.) Britannic Constitution. Folio. 4,50 London. *cf.* 1727

ACTON (T. H.) Reports of Cases before the Lords' Commissioners of Appeals in Prize Causes, &c., Vol. I. (all published.) 8vo. 4,00. London. 1811

ACTS AND LAWS of his Majesty's Province of Massachusetts Bay in New England. Folio. 1,00. Boston. 1759

ADAMS (John.) Treatise on the Principles and Practice of the Action of Ejectment, with Am. Notes and Precedents, by J. L. Tillinghast. 8vo. 4,50. New York. 1846

ADAMS (John, President.) Defence of the American Constitutions. 3 vols. 8vo. 6,50. Lond. 1794

ADDAMS (J.) See *Eng. Ecc. Reports*. 10,00. Lond. 1826

ADDISON (Alexander.) Reports of Cases in the County Courts of the Fifth Circuit, and in the High Court of Errors and Appeals in Pennsylvania. 2,00. Washington. 1800

ADOLPHUS (John Leycester.) See *Barnewall.*

AIKENS (Asa.) Reports of Cases in the Supreme Court of Vermont, from 1825 to 1828. 2 vols. 8vo. 7,50. Windsor, (Vt.) 1827

ALABAMA REPORTS. Reports of Cases at Law and in Equity, in the Supreme Court of Alabama. By the Judges of the Court. 8vo. 6 vols. 30,00. Tuskaloosa. 1841–4

ALDERSON (Edward Hall.) See *Barnewall.*

ALEYN (John.) Select Cases, Time of Charles I. Folio. 1,25. Lond. 1681

AMBLER (C.) Reports in Chancery, with some few in other Courts. 2d edit. with Corrections from the Registrar's Books, &c., References to subsequent Cases, a new Index, and a list of the Cases cited or referred to in the Text. By J. E. Blunt, Esq. 2 vols. royal 8vo. 7,50. London. 1828

AMERICAN CHANCERY DIGEST. See *Wheeler.*

AMERICAN JURIST and Law Magazine. New Series. 10 vols. 8vo. Boston. 12,50. 1838–42

The same, complete, 28 vols. *half cf.* 70,00. 1828

AMERICAN LAW JOURNAL and Miscellaneous Repertory, by John E. Hall. 6 vols. 8vo. 18,00. Philadelphia. 1808–17

AMERICAN STATE PAPERS. See *State.*

AMERICAN STATE PAPERS, and Public Documents of the United States from 1789 to 1818. 8vo. *calf.* 2,00. Boston. 1819

AMERICAN STATE PAPERS. Documents, Legislative and Executive, of the Congress of the United States; from the first session of the first Congress to the second session of the twenty-second Congress, (March 4, 1789, to March 2, 1833.) By Walter Lourie, Secretary of the Senate, and Matthew St. Clair Clark and Walter S. Franklin, Clerks of the House of Representatives. 21 vols. Folio. 120,00. Washington. 1834

AMES (Samuel.) See *Angell.*

AMICANGELO (J.) Questiones Feudales. Folio. 1,25. Naples. 1653

ANCIENT CHARTERS. See *Charters.*

ANDREWS (George.) Reports of Cases in the Court of King's Bench in the eleventh and twelfth Years of George II. Folio. 3,00. *cf.* London. 1754

ANGELL (Joseph K.) Treatise on the Limitation of Personal Actions founded upon Contracts. 2d ed. with Corrections and large Additions. (In press.)

ANGELL (Joseph K.) Treatise on the Common Law in relation to Water-Courses. With an Appendix, containing the principal adjudged Cases. 3d ed. With an Appendix, containing Forms and Declarations. 8vo. 3,00. Boston. 1840

ANGELL (Joseph K.) Law Intelligencer and Review. 3 vols. 8vo. 7,50. Providence and Philadelphia. 1828–31

ANGELL (Joseph K.) on Adverse Enjoyment. 8vo. 1,25. Boston. 1837

ANGELL (Joseph K.) A Practical Summary of the Law of Assignment. 12mo. 1,50. Boston. 1835

ANGELL (Joseph K.) and AMES (Samuel.) Treatise on the Law of Private Corporations Aggregate. 8vo. 3d ed. 5,50. Boston. 1846

The following extract from a letter of CHANCELLOR KENT to the authors, dated July 28th, 1843, shows the character of the work, and its great value to the profession:

"PERMIT ME TO SAY, THAT I THINK YOUR WORK IS NOT ONLY LABORIOUSLY, BUT FAITHFULLY, ACCURATELY, AND ADMIRABLY EXECUTED. IT IS A VERY LEARNED, FULL, AND FINISHED TREATISE, AND IT CANNOT BE TOO HIGHLY PRAISED. NO BRANCH OF THE SUBJECT APPEARS TO HAVE ESCAPED YOUR SKILFUL, CRITICAL, AND EXHAUSTING RESEARCHES."

ANSTRUTHER (Alexander.) Reports of Cases in the Exchequer from Mich. Term 32 Geo. III. to Trin. Term 37 Geo. III. 2 vols. 8vo. 8,50. London. 1796

ANTHON (John.) Reports of Cases at Nisi Prius in the Supreme Court of New York, with Notes on each Case, and an Introductory Essay on the Studies necessary to the Active Duties of the Bar. 8vo. 1,50. New York. 1820

ANTHON (John.) Digested Index to the Reported Decisions of the several Courts of Law in the United States. 8vo. 5 vols. 12,00. New York. 1813

ANTHON (John.) Notes on the Practice of the Supreme Court of New York. 8vo. ,75.

ANTROBUS (Rich.) and IMPEY (Thos.) See *Kitchen* (John.)

APPLETON (John.) Reports of Cases determined in the Supreme Judicial Court of the State of Maine. Vols. I. II. Being Vol. XIX. of the Maine Reports. 8vo. 4,00 a vol. Hallowell. 1842-3

ARCANA CLERICALIA, or the Mysteries of Clerkship Explained. 8vo. 1,00. London. 1705

ARCHBOLD (J. F.) Summary of Law and Pleading and Evidence in Criminal Cases, with Precedents of Indictments, with Notes by John Jervis. 8vo. 4,00. New York. 1840

ARCHBOLD (J. F.) Digest of the Law relative to Pleading and Evidence in Civil Actions. 2d Am. ed. 8vo. 4,00. New York. 1838

ARCHBOLD (J. F.) Law and Practice of Bankruptcy as founded on the recent Statute, with Forms. 12mo. 3d ed. By Flather. 3,00. London. 1829

ARCHBOLD (J. F.) The Practice of the King's Bench in Personal Actions and Ejectment. 2d American from the 2d London edition. 2 vols. 5,00. New York. 1838

ARCHBOLD (J. F.) The Law of Nisi Prius, comprising the Declarations and other Pleadings in Personal Actions, and the Evidence necessary to support them. 8vo. 2 vols. 5,00. Philadelphia. 1845

ARCHIVES de Droit et de Législation. 3 vols. 8vo. 9,00. Brussels. 1837

ARGON (M.) Institution au Droit Français. 2 vols. 12mo. 1,75. Paris. 1771

ASHE (Thomas.) General Table of Coke's Reports. 2 vols. 12mo. 3,75. London. 1618

ASHMEAD (John W.) Reports in Courts of Common Pleas, Quarter Sessions, Oyer and Terminer, and Orphan's Court of the First District of Pennsylvania. 8vo. 2 vols. Per vol. 5,00. Philadelphia. 1831-41

ATHERLY (E. G.) A Practical Treatise on the Law of Marriage and other Family Settlements. 8vo. 2,50. London. 1813

Atkyns (John Tracy.) Reports of Cases argued and determined in the High Court of Chancery, Temp. Hardwicke. 3 vols. Folio, *calf*. 7,50. London. 1765

Atkyns (John Tracy.) The Same, 3d ed. with Notes, by F. W. Sanders. 3 vols. 8vo. 12,00. New York. 1826

Attorney and Solicitor's Pocket-Book. By Jones. 7th ed. by Crisp. 2 vols. 5,50. London. 1841

Attorney's Practice in Courts of Common Pleas. 2 vols. 8vo. 2,50. London. 1758

Attorney's Practice in Courts of King's Bench. 2 vols. 8vo. 2,00. London. 1789

Attorney's and Agent's Table of Costs in the Courts of the King's Bench and Common Pleas, &c. &c. 4to. ,75 London. 1789

Ayliffe (John.) A New Pandect of Roman Civil Law, as anciently established in that Empire, and now received and practised in most European Nations. 7,50. Folio. London. 1734

Azuni (D. A.) Maritime Law of Europe. Translated from the French by William Johnson. 2 vols. 2vo. 3,00. New York. 1806

Bacon (Francis.) The Reading upon the Statutes of Uses. 8vo. 1,25. London. 1806

Bacon (Francis.) Law Tracts. 8vo. ,75. London. 1837

Bacon (Matthew.) The Complete Arbitrator, or the Law of Awards. 3d ed. 8vo. ,75 London. 1770

Bacon (Matthew.) Abridgment of the Law. 7th edition. Vols. 2d, 3d, and 4th (except the Addenda) by Henry Gwillim; vols. 1st, 5th, 6th, 7th, and 8th, and the Addenda to the other vols. by Charles Edward Dodd. 8 vols. 8vo. 50,00. London. 1832

Bacon (Matthew.) The Same. With the Notes and References made to the edition published in 1809, by Bird Wilson, Esq., to which are added Notes and References to

American Law Decisions, by John Bouvier. 10 vols. 8vo. 50,00. Philadelphia. 1842–6

BACON (Matthew.) The Same. 5 vols. 8vo. 10,00. Dublin. 1786

BACKUS (Joseph.) Digest of Laws relating to the Affairs and Duties of Sheriff, Coroner and Constable. 2 vols. 8vo. 4,50. New York. 1812

BACKUS (Joseph.) The Same. Second hand. 1,00.

BAGLEY (William.) New Practice in the Courts of Law at Westminster, with Forms embodied in the Text. 8vo. 7,00. London. 1840

BAILEY (H.) Reports of Cases in Equity, argued in the Court of Appeals of South Carolina. 8vo. 5,00. Charleston. 1841

BAILEY (H.) Reports of Cases in the Court of Appeals of S. C. on Appeal from the Courts of Law. 8vo. 2 vols. 10,00. Charleston. 1833

BAILEY (H.) Reports in the Court of Appeals of South Carolina. 8vo. 2 vols. 8,00. Charleston. 1833–4

BAILLY (M. A.) Administration Générale et Locale des Finances du Royaume-Uni. 2 vols. 8vo. 4,50. Paris. 1837

BAINBRIDGE (William.) A Practical Treatise on the Law of Mines and Minerals. 8vo. 5,00. London. 1841

BALDWIN (Henry.) Reports of Cases determined in the Circuit Court of the United States, in and for the Third Circuit. 8vo. 6,00. Philadelphia. 1837

BALL (Thomas) and BEATTY (Francis.) Reports of Cases argued and determined in the High Court of Chancery in Ireland, during the time of Lord Chancellor Manners; from the Sittings after Michaelmas Term, 48 George III. 1807, to the Sittings after Trinity Term, 51 George III. 1811. 2 vols. in 1. 5,00. Philadelphia. 1839

BALLANTINE (William.) Treatise on the Statute of Limitations. 8vo. 1,00. New York. 1812

BANKRUPTS, Laws relating to. 8vo. 1,50. London. 1791

BARBEYRAC (M.) Histoire des Anciens Traités ; ou Recueil Historique et Chronologique des Traites repandus dans les Auteurs Grecs et Latins et autres monumens de l'Antiquité, depuis les temps les plus reculés jusqu' à l'Empereur Charlemagne. Folio. *Neatly half bound.* 9,00. Amsterdam. 1739

BARBOUR (O. L.) and HARRINGTON (E. B.) Analytical Digest of the Equity Cases in all the United States Courts from the earliest period, and of the Decisions in Equity in England and Ireland since Hilary Term, 1822. 4 vols. 8vo. 13,00. Springfield. 1837–43

BARBOUR (O. L.) Treatise on the Law of Set-off, with an Appendix of Precedents. 8vo. 2,00. Albany. 1841

BARBOUR (O. L.) The Magistrate's Criminal Law, a Practical Treatise on Duty, &c., of Justices of the Peace in the State of New York in Criminal Cases. 8vo. Albany. 1841

BARBOUR (O. L.) A Treatise on the Practice of the Court of Chancery, with an Appendix of Precedents. 8vo. 2 vols. 14,00. New York. 1843

BARNARDISTON (Thomas.) Reports of Cases in the Court of King's Bench, together with some other Cases from Trin. 12 Geo. I. to Trin. 7 Geo. II. from 1726–31. Folio. 3,50. London. *cf. scarce.* 1744

BARNARDISTON (Thomas.) The Same. 8vo. *cf.* London. 1754

BARNES (Henry.) Notes of Points of Practice in Court of Common Pleas, from Mich. 1732, to Hil. 1756. 3d ed. 8vo. 5,00. Dublin. 1788

BARNHAM'S Series of Questions on the most Important Points connected with a Legal Education. 4th ed. enlarged. By Edward Ings, Esq., of the Inner Temple. 12mo. 1,75. London. 1840

BARNEWALL (R. V.) and ALDERSON'S (E. H.) Reports of Cases argued and determined in the Court of King's Bench, from Michaelmas, 58 Geo. III. 1817, to Trinity, 2 Geo. IV. 1824. 4 vols. royal 8vo. 12,00. Boston. 1822

BARTON (Charles, Jr.) Practical Points or Maxims in Conveyancing, being Selections from the Manuscripts of Mr. Butler, Mr. Preston, Mr. Bradley, Mr. Barton the Elder, the late Mr. Downing, and others. 8vo. 2,25. London. 1831

Barton (Charles.) Modern Precedents in Conveyancing, with Variations adapting them to different circumstances of Title. 3d ed. with great additions. 7 vols. royal 8vo. 17,50. London. 1821–4

Barrister (The.) By Ruggles. See *Ruggles.*

Basnage (Henri.) Œuvres de, contenant ses Commentaires sur la Coutûme de Normandie et son Traité des Hypotheques. 2 vols. Folio. *cf.* 7,50. Rouen. 1778

Bayard (Samuel.) Abstract of United States Laws on the Authority and Duties of Judges, &c. 8vo. 1,25. New York. 1834

Bayley (Sir John.) Summary of the Law of Bills of Exchange, Cash Bills, and Promissory Notes; from the 4th Lond. ed., with Notes by Willard Phillips and Samuel E. Sewall. 2d ed. 5,00. Boston. 1836

Baylies (Nicholas.) Digested Index to the Modern Reports of the Courts of Common Law in England and the United States. 3 vols. 8vo. 3,75. Montpelier, Vt.

Beames (John.) Sketch of the Doctrine relative to Commitments in Bankruptcy. 8vo. 1,75. London. 1827

Beaumont (George.) The Law of Fire and Life Insurance. 8vo. ,75. London. 1833

Beawes (Wyndham.) Lex Mercatoria. Folio. London. 3,00. 1771

Beawes (Wyndham.) Another Copy. Sixth Edition. Enlarged and Improved by J. Chitty. 2 vols. 4to. *cf.* 5,00. London. 1813

Beccaria on Crimes and Punishments; translated by Voltaire. 8vo. *cf.* 1,00. London. 1775

Becane (V.) Commentaire sur l'Ordonnance de la Marine du mois d'août 1681. 4to. 3,75. Poitiers. 1828

Beck (Theodrick R. and John B.) Elements of Medical Jurisprudence. 6th ed. 8vo. 7,50. Philadelphia. 1838

Bee (Thomas.) Reports of Cases adjudged in the District Court of South Carolina, to which is added an Appendix, containing Decisions in the Admiralty Court of Pennsylvania. By the late Thomas Hopkinson. 8vo. 4,00. Philadelphia. 1810

Beebe (P. O.) Questions adapted to Graham's Practice. 8vo. 2,00. New York. 1834

Belt (Robert.) Supplement to the Reports in Chancery of Francis Vesey, Sen., temp. Ld. Hardwicke. 8vo. 4,50 Philadelphia.

Benecke (Wm.) Treatise on the Principle of Indemnity in Marine Insurance, for the use of Underwriters, Merchants, and Lawyers. 8vo. 3,00. London. 1824

Benecke (William.) See *Stevens* and *Benecke*.

Benloe, (Gulielme, and Gulielme Dalison.) Les Reports des Divers Cases en le Court del Common-Bank, en le several Raignes de Hen. VII., Hen. VIII., Edward VI., Mar., et Eliz. Folio. 3,00. London. 1689

Bentham (J.) Traité des Preuves Judiciaires, par E. Dumont. 2 vols. 8vo. 4,50. Paris. 1830

Bentham (Jeremy.) Defence of Usury. 12mo. 4th ed. ,75. London. 1818

Berton (G. F. S.) Reports of Cases Adjudged in the Supreme Court of the Province of New Brunswick. 8vo. 2,00. Fredericton. 1835

Berton (G. F. S.) The same. 3,00. London. 1836

Berriat (Felix.) Notes Élémentaires sur le Code Civil. 8vo. 2 vols. *cf.* 4,50. Paris. 1845

Bills of Costs and Allowances as between Party and Party in the Court of Common Pleas, &c. 8vo. *bds.* 1,00. London. 1829

Binkershoek (Cornelii Van.) Opera Omnia edidit et præfatus est B. Phillipus Vicat. 2 vols. in 1. Folio. *old cf.* 5,00. 1761

Binkershoek (Cornelius Van.) Law of War. 1 vol. 8vo. 1,25. Philadelphia. 1810

BINNEY (Horace.) Reports of Cases adjudged in the Supreme Court of Pennsylvania. 6 vols. 8vo. 24,00. Philadelphia. 1809–12

BIOCHE et GOUJET, Dictionnaire de la Procédure Civile et Commerciale. 5 vols. 8vo. 12,50. Paris. 1839

BIRD (James Barry.) Supplement to Mr. Barton's Modern Precedents. 8vo. 2,00. London.

BIRD (J. B.) Law Selections, containing Treatises upon such Heads and Divisions of the Law as are of most general Use and Importance. 2 vols. 8vo. 1805–8

BIRD (J. B.) New Pocket Conveyancer, or Attorney's complete Pocket-book; comprising a choice Selection and great Variety of the most valuable and approved Precedents in Conveyancing; in which the Modern Forms introduced by Conveyancers of the highest eminence now in practice are particularly attended to, and the Efficacy of them explained; to which are also added, Preliminary Observations relative to the Nature and Use of each particular species of Deed. 5th ed. 2 vols. small 12mo. 1,50. London. 1830

BISSET (Andrew.) A Practical Treatise on the Law of Estates for Life. 8vo. 2,50. London. 1842

BLACKFORD (Isaac.) Reports of Cases Argued and Determined in the Superior Court of the State of Indiana from May, 1817, to May, 1826. 8vo. 5,00. Indianapolis. 1830

BLACKSTONE (Sir William.) Commentaries on the Laws of England, with Notes. By Christian, Archbold, and Chitty, with the Analysis of Baron Field. 2 vols. 8vo. 4,00. New York. 1845

BLACKSTONE (Sir W.) The same, with the last Corrections of the Author, and Notes by John Taylor Coleridge, Esq. 16th ed. 4 vols. 12,00. London. 1825

BLACKSTONE (Sir W.) The same. By Stewart. 4 vols. 8vo. 16,00. London. 1844

BLACKSTONE (Sir W.) The same. By Hovenden and Ryland. vols. 8vo. 12,00. London. 1836

BLACKSTONE (Sir W.) The same. 12th ed. By Chitty. 4 vols. 4,00. London. 1793

BLACKSTONE (H.) Reports in Common Pleas and Exchequer, from East. Term, 28 Geo. III. 1788, to Hil. Term, 36 Geo. III. 1796. 4th ed., with Notes, &c. 2 vols. royal 8vo. 7,50. 1827

BLACKSTONE (Sir W.) Reports in K. B. & C. P., from 1746 to 1779; with numerous additional Notes, References, and an entire New and copious Index. By C. H. Elsley, Esq. 2 vols. royal 8vo. 7,50. 1828

BLANEY (Frederick.) A Practical Treatise on Life Annuities. 8vo. ,75. London. 1817

BLAXLAND (George.) Digest of the Principles of English Law, arranged in the order of the Code Napoleon. 8vo. 8,50. London. 1839

BLOUNT (Thomas.) Fragmenta Antiquitatis, or Ancient Tenures of Land and Jocular Customs of Manors, enlarged and corrected by Beckwith. 4to. 9,00. London. 1815

BLUNT (Joseph.) Shipmaster's Assistant and Commercial Digest. 8vo. 4,00. 1837

BLYDENBURGH (J. W.) Treatise on the Law of Usury. 8vo. 3,50. New York. 1844

BOHUN (W.) Declarations and Pleadings in the most usual Actions. 8vo. 2,00. London. 1733

BOHUN (W.) Rights, Liberties, Privileges, Laws and Customs of the City of London. 8vo. 1,25. London. 1723

BOILEUX (J. M.) Commentaire sur le Code Civil, revu par M. F. F. Poncelet. 3 vols. 8vo. 7,50. Paris. 1842

BOITARD. Code de la Procédure Civile, publié par Gustave de Linage. Vol. 1. 2,25. Bruxelles. 1840

BOLTON (Geo.) Practice of the Criminal Courts, including the Proceedings before Magistrates in Petty and Quarter Sessions and at the Assizes. 12mo. *cf.* 2,50. London. 1835

BONCENNE (M.) Théorie de la Procédure Civile. 2 vols. 8vo. 4,00. Bruxelles. 1839

BONJEAN (M. L. B.) Institutes de L'Empereur Justinien, Traduites en Français. 8vo. 2 vols. 3,00. Paris. 1838

BONNIER (M. E.) Traité Théorique et Pratique des Preuves en Droit Civil et en Droit Criminel. 8vo. Half *cf.* 2,75. Paris. 1843

BOOTH (George.) Nature and Practice of Real Actions. 8vo. 1,50. London. 1811

BOOTH (R.) Historical Treatise of an Action or Suit at Law, &c. 8vo. 1,00. London. 1823

BOSANQUET (J. B.) and PULLER'S (C.) Reports in the Court of Common Pleas and Exchequer Chamber, and in the House of Lords, from Easter Term, 36 G. III. 1796, to Trinity Term, 47 G. III. 1807. The 3d ed., with Notes, and References. 5 vols. royal 8vo. 13,50. London. 1826

Another Copy. Second hand. 4 vols. 8vo. 9,50. Philadelphia. 1804

BOSCAWEN (William.) Treatise on Convictions on Penal Statutes. 12mo. 1,50. Dublin. 1792

BOSSANGE (Ad.) Des Crimes et des Peines Capitales. 8vo. 1,50. Paris. 1832

BOULAY-PATY. (P. S.) Traité des Assurances et des Contrats à la grosse d'Emérigon. 2 vols. 4to. 6,00. Paris. 1827

BOULAY-PATY. Cours de Droit Commercial Maritime. 2 vols. 8vo. 4,00. Bruxelles. 1838

BOUSQUET, (J.) Dictionnaire des Contrats et Obligations en Matière Civile et Commerciale. 2 vols. 8vo. 4,50. Paris. 1840

BOUSQUET (J.) Nouveau Dictionnaire de Droit, resumé générale de la Legislation, &c. 2 vols. 8vo. Half *cf.* 7,50. Paris. 1844

BOUVIER (John.) A Law Dictionary adapted to the Constitution and Laws of the U. S. A. and the several States, with reference to the Civil and other Systems of Foreign Law. 2 vols. 8vo. 9,00. Philadelphia. 1840

BRACKENRIDGE (H. M.) Essay on Trusts and Trustees. 8vo. 2,00. Washington. 1842

BRADBY (James.) Treatise on the Law of Distresses. 1st

Am. ed. from the London ed. of 1808. 8vo. 2,00. New York. 1808

Brady (J. H.) Plain Advice to the Public to facilitate the making of their own Wills, with Forms of Wills, simple and elaborate, Tables of the Stamp Duties on Probates and Letters of Administration. 4th ed. 8vo. 1,00 London. 1838

Breese (Sidney.) Reports of Cases in the Supreme Court of Illinois — 1819 to 1830. 3,00. Kaskaskia. 1831

Brice (John.) Laws of the U. S. now in force relative to Commercial Subjects. 8vo. 1,50. Baltimore. 1831

Bridgman (Sir Orl.) Conveyances; being Select Precedents of Deeds and Instruments concerning the most considerable Estates in England. Folio. *old cf.* 1,25. London. 1682

Bridgman (Richard Whalley.) Rules and Principles of the Law of Nisi Prius. 8vo. 1,50. New York. 1811

Brigham (Wm.) The Charter and Laws of the Colony of New Plymouth. Published agreeably to a Resolve of the Massachusetts Legislature, April 5, 1836. 8vo. 1,50. Boston. 1836

British Crown Cases. See *Moody*, *Russell*, *Ryan*, and *Jebb*.

Brockenbrough (John W.) Reports of Cases decided by the Hon. John Marshall, late Chief Justice of the United States, in the Circuit Court of the United States for the District of Virginia and North Carolina, from 1802 to 1833. 2 vols. 8vo. 10,00. *cf.* Philadelphia. 1837

Brougham (Henry, Lord.) An Inquiry into the Colonial Policy of the European Powers. 2 vols. 8vo. 12,00. London. 1803

Browne (Arthur.) View of the Civil Law and of the Law of Admiralty. 2d ed. 2 vols. 8vo. 7,00. New York. 1840

Browne (Peter A.) Reports of Cases in the Court of Common Pleas of the First Judicial District of Pennsylvania. 2 vols. 8vo. 6,00. Philadelphia. 1811

Brown (William.) Reports of Cases argued and determined in the High Court of Chancery, during the time of Lord Chancellor Thurlow, and of the several Lords Commissioners of the Great Seal, and Lord Chancellor Loughborough, from 1778 to 1794. By William Brown, Esq., of the Inner Temple, Barrister at Law. First American from the fifth London edition; with important Corrections and Additions, from the Registrar's Books; from the Author's Manuscript Notes in his own copy, intended for a further edition; from various Manuscript Notes of the highest authority, by eminent contemporary and dignified members of the profession; together with all the Notes and References, by Robert Belt, Esq., of the Inner Temple, Barrister at Law; and many valuable Notes by the Hon. Robert Henley Eden, of Lincoln's Inn, Barrister at Law. To which are now added copious Notes and References to American and later English Cases, by J. C. Perkins, Esq. 4 vols. 8vo. 14,00. Boston. 1844

Brown (J.) Reports of Cases upon Appeals and Writs of Error in the High Court of Parliament, from 1751 to 1800. 8 vols. 8vo. 12,00. Dublin. 1784

Brownlow (Richard.) Book of Entries, contained in Brownlow's Declarations, now published in Latin, the original language. Folio. 3,50. London. 1693

Bullard (H. A.) and Curry (T.) New Digest of the Statute Laws of the State of Louisiana, from the Change of Government to the year 1841, inclusive. Vol. I. 8vo. 5,00. New Orleans. 1842

Buller (Sir Francis.) Introduction to the Law relative to Trials at Nisi Prius. 4to. 2,00. *cf.* London. 1772

Buller (Sir Francis.) The same. 8vo. 1,25.

Bunbury (William.) Reports of Cases in the Court of Exchequer from the beginning of the Reign of George I. to the 14th George II. 2d ed. 8vo. 1,50. Dublin. 1793

Burke (Edmund.) Works of. 9 vols. 8vo. 12,00. Boston. 1839

"The present edition of Burke's works is more complete than any one which has hitherto appeared either in England or America. It comprises the entire contents of the English edition of his works, in sixteen octavo volumes, including two volumes of Speeches on the Trial of Hastings, published in 1827, and which have never before been republished in this country. It also contains a reprint of the work entitled 'An Account of the European Settlements in America,' first published in 1761, which, though published anonymously, is well known to have been written by Burke, and also the correspondence with French Laurence, which are not contained in the English edition of his collected works. Although the present edition contains a volume more than the latest and best English one, it is offered at less than one half the price. It has been the aim of the publishers to present the work in a form and style worthy of its contents; and it is confidently offered to the favorable regard of the public from its completeness, its moderate price, and its typographical excellence." — *Preface to the Edition.*

"The publishers of this edition have borne in mind the nature and value of the contents, and given the mechanical execution a degree of excellence corresponding to the literary and political merits of the volumes, of which there are nine, in octavo, containing all that is given in the sixteen octavo volumes of the London edition, and including two volumes on the East India Question, and an account of the European discovery in America, which last is not in the London edition.

"This edition of Burke may be considered as containing all that that distinguished writer intended for the press, and is commended to the taste and judgment of those who are forming or completing a library." — *United States (Philadelphia) Gazette.*

"Possessed of most extensive knowledge, and of the most various description; acquainted alike with what different classes of men knew, each in his own province, and with much that hardly any one ever thought of learning, he could either bring his masses of information to bear directly upon the subjects to which they severally belonged — or he could avail himself of them generally to strengthen his faculties and enlarge his views — or he could turn any portion of them to account for the purpose of illustrating his theme, or enriching his diction. Hence, when he is handling any one matter, we perceive that we are conversing with a reasoner or teacher, to whom almost every other branch of knowledge is familiar. His views range over all cognate subjects; his reasonings are derived from principles applicable to other matters as well as the one in hand; arguments pour in from all sides, as well as those which start up under our feet, the natural growth of the path he is leading us over; while to throw light round our steps, and either explore its darker places, or serve for our recreation, illustrations are fetched from a thousand quarters; and an imagination marvellously quick to descry unthought-of resemblances, pours forth the stores which a lore much more marvellous has gathered from all ages, and nations, and arts, and tongues. We are, in respect of the argument, reminded of Bacon's multifarious knowledge, and the exuberance of his learned fancy; while the many-lettered diction recalls to mind the first of English poets, and his immortal verse, rich with the spoils of all sciences and all times." — *Lord Brougham. Sketches of English Statesmen.*

Burlamaqui (J. J.) Principles of Natural and Politic Law, translated into English by Mr. Nugent. 2 vols. 8vo. *cf.* 3,50. London. 1763

Burn (R.) Justice of the Peace and Parish Officer. 27th ed., with Corrections and Additions. The Criminal and Poor Law, edited by Mr. Serjeant D'Oyly, and the remaining Titles, by E. V. Williams. 5 vols. 8vo. 20,00. London. 1836

Burn (R.) Ecclesiastical Law, the 9th ed., corrected, with very considerable Additions, including the Statutes Cases to the Present Time. By Charles Durnford, Esq., Advocate in Doctor's Commons, Barrister of the Middle Temple, &c. &c. 5 vols. 8vo. *bds.* 10,00. 1810

Burn (R.) The same, with additions. By Tyrwhitt. 4 vols. 12,00. London. 1824

Burrow (Sir James.) Report of Cases in King's Bench, 30 Geo. II. 1756, to East. 12 Geo. III. 1772. 4th ed. 5 vols. 8vo. 12,00. New York. 1833

Burrow (Sir James.) The same. 5 vols. 10,00. Dublin. 1794

Burrow (Sir James.) The same. 2 vols. condensed. 8vo. 7,00. New York. 1833

Burrow (Sir James.) Decisions of King's Bench upon Settlement Cases, from March, 1732, to June, 1768. 3 vols. 4to. 7,50. London. 1768

Burrow (Sir James.) The same work in 1 vol. 8vo. 3,00. Dublin. 1790

Burton (W. H.) An Elementary Compendium of the Law of Real Property. 8vo. 2,00. Philadelphia. 1839

Burton (John Hill.) Manual of the Law of Scotland, Civil,

Municipal, Criminal and Ecclesiastical. 12mo. 3,00. Edinburgh. 1839

BUTLER (Charles.) Horæ Juridicæ Subsecivæ. 8vo. ,75. Philadelphia. 1808

BYNKERSHOEK (C. Van.) Treatise on the Law of War, with Notes. By P. S. Du Ponceau. 8vo. 1,25. Phil. 1810

BYNKERSHOEK (C. Van.) Opera Omnia. Folio. *cf.* 7,50 Leyden. 1767

CAINES (George.) Summary of the Practice in the Supreme Court of the State of New York. 8vo. 1,00. New York. 1808

CAINES (George.) Cases in the Court for the Trial of Impeachments and Correction of Errors in the State of New York. 2 vols. in 1. 5,00. New York. 1805

CALDECOTT (Thomas.) Reports of Cases relative to the Duty and Office of Justice of the Peace from 1776 to 1785. 8vo. 2,50. London. 1790

CALDWELL (James Stamford.) Treatise on the Law of Arbitration, with an Appendix of Precedents. 1st Am. ed. With a Digested Index of American Decisions. 8vo. 3,00. Exeter. 1822

CAMERON (Duncan) and NORWOOD (Wm.) Reports of Cases ruled and determined by the Court of Conference of North Carolina. 8vo. 3,00. Raleigh. 1805

CAMPBELL (John.) Reports of Cases at Nisi Prius, in King's Bench and Common Pleas, from Mich. 48 Geo. III. 1807, to Hil. 51 Geo. III. 1816. 8,00. New York. 1810–11

CAREY (Henry.) Treatise on the Law of Partnership, with Precedents of Deeds. 8vo. 2,00. London. 1827

CAREY (Henry.) Commentary on the Tenures of Littleton, written prior to Coke on Littleton. Edited from a copy in the Harleian Collection. 8vo. 3,00. London. 1829

CAREY (Henry.) Laws of Juries. 12mo. ,50. Lond. 1826

CAROLINA (The.) Law Repository. 2 vols. 8vo. 12,00. Raleigh. 1814–16

CARY (Sir G.) Reports in Chancery, whereunto is annexed the King's Order and Decree in Chancery for a Rule to be observed in that Court. 12mo. 1,25. London. 1820

CARTER (S.) Reports of Cases argued in the Court of Common Pleas, in the 16th, 17th, 18th and 19th Years of Charles II. Folio. *cf.* 2,50. London. 1688

CASES adjudged in the Court of King's Bench, concerning Settlements and Removals, from the first year of Geo. I. to the present time. 12mo. 1,00. London. 1742

CASES of Privilege of Parliament, from the earliest Records to the year 1628. 4to. *bds.* 2,25. London. 1776

CASES adjudged in the Court of King's Bench, from the 2d year of William III. to the end of his Reign. Folio. *bds.* 2,00. London. 1738

CASES in the High Court of Chancery, from the 12th year of Charles II. to the 31st. Folio. 2,00. London. 1697

CASES in Chancery, Temp. Car. II. and Jac. II. Folio. *cf.* 2,00. London. 1707

CASES in Chancery, Temp. Car. II. and Jac. II. 3 Parts. Pt. 1st, 3d ed., pt. 2d, 2d ed., pt. 3d, 4th ed. 8vo. 3,50. New York. 1828

CASES Temp. Hardwicke, in K. B. 7, 8, 9, and 10 Geo. II.; to which are added some Determinations of the Lord Chief Justice, &c. 2d. ed. By T. Lee, Esq. Royal 8vo. 3,50. London. 1815

This is cited as Annaly's Reports.

CASES argued and decided in the High Court of Chancery. From the 2d London edition. 8vo. 3,50. N. York. 1828.

CASES relating to Railways and Canals in Law and Equity. By Carrow and Oliver. 2 vols. 8vo. 12,00. Lon. 1841-4

CASES, with Opinions of eminent Counsel, in matters of Law, Equity and Conveyancing. 2 vols. 8vo. 3,00. London. 1791

CASES in Chancery in the Reign of Charles I., Charles II., and James II. 2 vols. 8vo. 9,00. London. 1715

CASTILLO SOTOMAVYOR (John del.) Opera Omnia. Folio. 11 vols. 20,00. Cologne (France.) 1727

CAUSES Célèbres, Recueil des, et des Arrêts qui les ont decidés. 23 vols. 8vo. *cf.* 23,00. Paris. 1807

CELEBRATED Trials of all Countries, and remarkable Cases of Criminal Jurisprudence. 2,00. Philadelphia. 1836

CENTRAL Criminal Court Cases. Minutes of Evidence taken by Henry Buckler. 5 vols. 8vo. *cf.* 20,00. London. 1835

CHARLTON (R. M.) Reports of Decisions made in the Superior Courts of the Eastern District of Georgia. 8vo. 5,00. Savannah. 1838

CHARLTON (T. U. P.) Reports in the Superior Courts of the Eastern District of the State of Georgia. 8vo. 2,00. New York. 1824

CHARTER granted by Wm. and Mary to the Inhabitants of Massachusetts Bay — also the Laws of Massachusetts Bay from 1692 to 1762. Folio. 1,50. Boston, N. E. 1759

CHARTER of Dartmouth College, with general Outline of the Argument in the Case of Dartmouth College *v.* Woodward. 8vo. 1,00. Hanover. 1816

CHARTERS and General Laws of Massachusetts Bay, collected from Public Records and Ancient Printed Books, with an Appendix, explaining the Spirit, Progress and History of the Jurisprudence of the State. Published by order of the General Court. 8vo. 5,00. Boston. 1814

> *Commonwealth of Massachusetts. In the House of Representatives, Jan. 15th,* 1812. RESOLVED, That the Hon. NATHAN DANE, WILLIAM PRESCOTT and JOSEPH STORY, Esquires, be a committee, at the expense of the Commonwealth, to collect the Charters and the public and general Laws of the late colony and province of Massachusetts Bay."

CHASE (Salmon P.) Statutes of Ohio and the North-Western Territory, adopted or enacted from 1788 to 1833, inclusive, together with the Ordinance of 1787. 3 vols. 8vo. 18,00. Cincinnati. 1833

CHASE (Samuel.) Associate Justice of the Supreme Court of the United States. Trial of, before the House of Representatives. 2 vols. 8vo. 4,00. Washington. 1805

Chipman (Daniel.) Essay on the Law of Contracts for the Payment of Specific Articles. 8vo. 1,25. Middlebury, Vt. 1822

Chipman (Daniel.) Reports of Cases in the Supreme Court of Vermont. 2 vols. 8vo. 3,75. Middlebury. 1824

Chipman (Daniel.) Principles of Government, a Treatise on Free Institutions. 8vo. 2,50. Burlington. 1833

Chitty (Joseph.) Practical Treatise on Bills of Exchange and Promissory Notes; a new edition, with Notes, &c. 8vo. 5,00. Springfield. 1842

Chitty (Joseph.) Treatise on the Parties to Actions, the Form of Actions, and on Pleading, with a second vol. of Precedents of Pleadings. 3 vols. 8vo. 10,00. Springfield. 1844

Chitty (Joseph.) Practical Treatise on the Law of Nations, relative to the Legal Effect of War on the Commerce of Belligerents and Neutrals, and on Orders in Council and Licenses. 8vo. 1,50. Boston. 1812

Chitty (Joseph.) Treatise on Criminal Law; comprising the Practicc, Pleading, and Evidence in a Criminal Prosecution, with a Collection of Precedents; Notes by Peters and Huntington, and references to American Cases, by J. C. Perkins. 3 vols. 8vo. 9,00. Brookfield. 1836

Chitty (Joseph.) On the Stamp Laws. 12mo. 2,25. London. 1829

Chitty (Joseph.) Practice of the Law in all its Departments. 4 vols. 8vo. 16,00. Philadelphia. 1834–9

Chitty (Joseph.) Practical Treatise on Medical Jurisprudence. 8vo. 3,00. Philadelphia. 1836

Chitty (Joseph, Jr.) Practical Treatise on the Law of Contracts not under Seal, and upon the Usual Defences to Actions thereon. Notes by J. C. Perkins. 4th Am. ed. 8vo. 5,00. Springfield. 1844

Chitty (Joseph, Jr.) Precedents in Pleading, with copious Notes on Practice, Pleading and Evidence. Edited by Henry Pearson and Thompson Chitty. 2 vols. 8vo. 5,00. Springfield. 1839

CHITTY (Joseph, Jr.) Practical Treatise on Bills of Exchange, Promissory Notes and Bankers' Checks; containing Forms of Affidavits of Debt in Action thereon, and of Declarations and Pleas on such Actions, adapted to the New Rules on Pleading, with an Appendix of all the Statutes, and decided Cases, in *full*, from the earliest period to the present time, relating to Bills and Notes, the Bank of England and Bankers. 2 vols. royal 8vo. 7,50. London. 1834

CHITTY (Joseph, Jr.) Treatise on the Law of the Prerogatives of the Crown, and the relative Duties and Rights of the Subject. 8vo. 3,75. London. 1820

CHITTY (Edward.) Index to all the Reported Cases, Statutes and General Orders in or relating to the Principles, Pleading and Practice of Equity and Bankruptcy in the several Courts in England, from the earliest period to 1831. 2 vols. 8vo. 10,00. Philadelphia. 1831

CHRISTIAN (Edward.) Origin, Progress and present Practice of the Bankrupt Law in England and Ireland. 2d ed. 2 vols. 8vo. 11,00. London. 1818

CITY HALL. New York Recorder, containing Reports of the various Trials of the City Courts, from 1816 to 1821. 6 vols. in 3. 9,00. New York. 1816–21

CIVIL CODE of the State of Louisiana, with Annotations by W. S. Upton and N. R. Jennings. In French and English. 8vo. 5,50. New Orleans. 1838

CLANCY (James.) Treatise on the Rights, Duties and Liabilities of Husband and Wife at Law and in Equity. 2d Am. ed. 8vo. 3,50. New York. 1837

CLERKE (Thomas W.) A Practical Elementary Digest of the Reported Cases in the Supreme Court of Judicature and the Court for the Correction of Errors of the State of New York, &c. 2 vols. 8vo. 15,00. New York. 1841

CLERKE (Thomas W.) Rudiments of American Law and Practice, on the Plan of Blackstone, prepared for the use of Students at Law, &c. 1 vol. 8vo. 3,50. New York. 1842

CLIFT (Henry.) New Book of Entries, Digested and Published by Sir Charles Ingleby. Folio. 3,00. *half cf.* London. 1719

COBBETT's Parliamentary History of England, from the Norman Conquest, in 1066, to the year 1803. 36 vols. 8vo. *Neat half Russia.* 70,00. London. 1806

COCKBURN (William.) Clerk's Assistant in the Practice of the Ecclesiastical Courts, with Appendixes, containing a Summary of the Method of Proceeding in the Ecclesiastical Courts, a Collection of the Modern Rules of Practice and Cases adjudged in Doctors' Commons, and a List of Fees in the Consistory Court, &c. 4th ed. 8vo. 3,00. Dublin. 1792

CODE des Prises, ou Recueil des Édits Declaratoires, etc. etc. dépuis 1400 jusqu' à présent. 4to. 2 vols. 5,00. Paris. 1784

CODE (The.) Napoleon, or the French Civil Code, translated from the original and official edition published at Paris, 1804. By a Barrister of the Inner Temple. 8vo. 3,50. New York. 1841

CODE CIVIL. Motifs et Discours prononcés lors de la Publication du Code Civil, par les divers Orateurs du Conseil d'État et du Tribunal. Royal 8vo. 2 vols. 7,50. Paris. 1838

COKE (Sir Edward.) Book of Entries, containing approved Precedents, collected and published for the common good and benefit of all the Studious and Learned Professors of the Laws of England. Folio. "Best edition." 7,50. London. 1614

COKE (Sir Edward.) The same. Injured binding. 5,50.

COKE (Sir Edward.) The First Part of the Institutes of the Laws of England. 11th ed. Folio. 2,50. London. 1719

COKE (Sir Edward.) The First Part of the Institutes of the Laws of England, or a Commentary upon Littleton; not the Name of the Author only, but of the Law itself. 15th ed. By Hargrave and Butler. Including the Notes of Hale and Lord Chancellor Nottingham, and the second, third and fourth parts of the Institutes. 8vo. 7 vols. *cf.* 28,00. London. 1794–7

COKE (Sir Edward.) First, Second and Third Parts of the Institutes of the Laws of England, or a Commentary upon

Littleton ; not the Name of a Lawyer only, but of the Law itself. 3 vols. Folio. 7,00. London. 1633

Coke (Sir Edward.) Systematic Arrangement of his First Institute on the Plan of Lord Hale's Analysis, with the Annotations of Mr. Hargrave, Lords Hale and Nottingham, and New Notes and References, by J. H. Thomas. 1st Am. ed., from the last London ed.; to which are added the Notes of Charles Butler. 3 vols. 8vo. 12,00. Philadelphia. 1836

Coke (Sir Edward.) The same. 3 vols. 8vo. *bds.* 7,50. London. 1815

Coke (Sir Edward.) Reports in Verse. 18mo. ,25. London. 1825

Coke (Sir Edward.) Abridgment of the Eleven Books of his Reports, by Sir Thomas Ireland; also the Twelfth and Thirteenth Books, by John A. Dunlap. 8vo. 3,00. New York. 1813

Coke (Sir Edward.) Reports from 14th Eliz. to the 13th Jas. 11 Parts, in 3 vols. Folio. Complete. 7,50. *cf.* London. 1601–16

Coke (Sir Edward.) Reports in 13 Parts complete, revised by George Wilson, Serjeant at Law. 8vo. 15,00. Dublin. 1793

Coke (Sir Edward.) The same. New edition. By Thomas J. H. and Frazer J. F. 6 vols. 8vo. 25,00. London. 1826

Collectanea Juridica, consisting of Tracts relative to the Law and Constitution of England. 2 vols. 8vo. 2,50. London.

Collection des Constitutions, Chartes et Lois Fondamentales des Peuples de l'Europe et des deux Ameriques, avec des Précis offrant l'Histoire des Libertés et des Institutions Politiques chez les nations modernes; et une Table alphabetique raisonée des matières; MM. P.-A. Dufau; J.-B. Duvergier et J. Guadet. 6 vols. 8vo. 12,00. Paris. 1823

Collection of Interrogatories for the Examination of Witnesses in Courts of Equity. 12mo. 2,50. Dublin. 1791

Colles (Richard.) Reports of Cases, 1697—1713. 2,00. 8vo. Dublin. 1789

Collinson (G. D.) Treatise on the Law concerning Idiots, Lunatics, and other Persons Non Compotes Mentis. 2 vols. 8vo. 7,00. London. 1812

Collyer (John.) Practical Treatise on the Law of Partnership. With Notes of American Cases, by Willard Phillips and Edward Pickering. 8vo. 3,50. Springfield. 1839

Colman and Caines's Cases of Practice in the Supreme Court of New York from 1794 to 1805. 8vo. 3,00. New York. 1808

Comberbach (Roger.) Reports of Cases in King's Bench, from 1st Jac. II. to 10 Wm. III. Folio. 3,00. London. 1724

Commentaires sur la Coutume de Normandie, par Berault et Godefroy, et la Paraphrase de M. d'Aviron. Folio. 2 vols. 9,50. Rouen. 1776

Commentaire Nouveau sur les Ordonnances d'Août, 1669, et Mars, 1673. 12mo. 1,00. Paris. 1761

Commentary and Review of Montesquieu's Spirit of Laws. 8vo. 1,25. Philadelphia. 1811

Commentary on the Tenures of Littleton, written prior to the publication of Coke upon Littleton, edited from a copy in the Harleian Collections of Manuscripts. By Henry Carey. 8vo. 4,50. London. 1829

Commercial Report. Report of the great Commercial Cause of Minet and Fector *v.* Gibson and Johnson, decided in the House of Lords, 1791, including the Speeches of Lord Kenyon, Lord Loughborough, &c. &c. 8vo. 1,25. London. 1791

Common Law. See *Law*.

Compendium (A) of the Practice in the Court of Exchequer, at Westminster. 8vo. 1,25. London. 1688

Comstock (Franklin G.) Digest of the Law of Executors and Administrators, Guardian and Ward, and Dower. 8vo. 3,50. Hartford. 1832

COMTE (Charles.) Traité de Législation ou Exposition des Lois Générales. 8vo. 2,50. Brussels. 1837

COMYN (R. B.) Treatise on the Law of Usury. 8vo. 1,25. London. 1817

COMYN (Samuel.) Law of Contracts and Promises upon various Subjects and with particular Persons, as settled in the Action of Assumpsit. 1st Am. from 2d London ed. 8vo. 4,00. New York. 1835

COMYNS (Sir John.) Digest of the Laws of England, 5th edition, to which is added a Digest of the Cases at Nisi Prius, by Anthony Hammond, Esq. 8 vols. 8vo. *cf.* 48,00. London. 1822

COMYNS (Sir John.) Reports of Cases in King's Bench, Common Pleas and Exchequer. Folio. 4,00. London. 1744

COMYNS (Sir John.) The same. 2d ed. With Notes, by Rose. 2 vols. 8vo. 7,00. London. 1792

CONDENSED Reports of Cases in the Court of Chancery in England, from 1820 to 1845. Edited by Richard Peters, and E. D. Ingraham. 17 vols. 8vo. 4,50. per vol. Philadelphia and New York. 1831–45

CONDENSED Reports of Cases in the Supreme Court of the United States, containing the whole Series of the Decisions of the Court from its organization to the commencement of Peters's Reports, 1827. Edited by Richard Peters. 6 vols. 8vo. 24,00. Philadelphia. 1841

CONDENSED Reports. Supreme Court U. States, 1834–5, by William Cranch, and Richard Cox. 8vo. 3,00. Washington. 1835

CONDENSED Reports of Cases in the Superior Court of the Territory of New Orleans, and in the Supreme Court of Louisiana, containing the Decisions of those Courts from the Autumn Term, 1809, to the March Term, 1830, and which were embraced in the 20 vols. of Martin's Reports, with Notes, &c. By J. Burton Harrison. 4 vols. 8vo. 24,00. New Orleans. 1839

CONDORCET (M.) Commentary on Montesquieu. 8vo. 1,25. Philadelphia. 1822

CONDUCTOR Generalis, being the Law relative to Justices of the Peace. 8vo. 2,00. Albany. 1819

CONGRESSIONAL Debates. A Register of Debates in Congress, from 1824 to 1828. (Gales & Seaton's,) 4 vols. 8vo. 10,00. Washington. 1825–9

CONKLIN (Alfred.) Treatise on the Organization, Jurisdiction and Practice of the Courts of the United States. 2d ed. 8vo. 4,50. New York. 1842

CONNECTICUT Reports. See *Day.*

CONOVER (J. F.) Digested Index of all the Reported Decisions in Law and Equity of the Supreme Courts of the States of Ohio, Indiana, and Illinois. 8vo. 4,00. Philadelphia. 1834

CONSISTORY Reports. See *Haggard.*

CONSULTATIONES Saxonicæ. Folio. 3,00. Francfort. 1616

CONVEYANCER'S Light, or Precedents for all manner of Instruments. Composed by the advice of many eminent Lawyers. 3d ed. 4to. 4,00. London. 1671

COOKE (William.) Bankrupt Laws. 4th ed. 2 vols. 8vo. 6,00. London. 1799

COOKE (William.) A compendious System of the Bankrupt Laws. 8vo. *cf.* ,75. Dublin. 1786

COOPER (George.) Cases in Chancery, in Hil., East., and Trin., 55 Geo. III., 1815. 8vo. 3,50. New York. 1824

COOPER (Judge.) Opinion of, on the Effect of a Sentence of a Foreign Court of Admiralty. 8vo. 1,00. Philadelphia. 1810

COOPER (Thomas.) See *Statutes of South Carolina.*

COOPER (C. P.) Lettres sur la Cour de la Chancellerie et quelques Points de la Jurisprudence Anglaise. Nouv. ed. 8vo. 2,50. London. 1828

CORPUS Juris Civilis, cum notis D. Gothofredi, etc. 2 vols. Imp. folio. *neat half calf.* 13,50. Vitray. 1728

CORPUS Juris Civilis. The same, in 2 vols. Folio. *neat half calf.* 11,00.

CORPUS Juris Civilis. The same. 2 vols. 4to. *half bd.* 8,50. Lipsiæ. 1705

CORPUS Juris Civilis. The same. With Notes, &c., by Hermann and A. and M. Kriegel. 3 vols. royal 8vo. *half cf.* 9,00. Leipsic. 1833–44

COTTON (Sir Robert.) An exact Abridgment of the Records in the Tower of London, from Ed. II. to Richard III. Folio. *cf.* 5,75. London. 1687

COVENTRY (Thomas) and HUGHES (Samuel.) Digested Index to the Common Law Reports, from Hen. III. 1272, to Geo. III. 1760. 2 vols. 8vo. 7,50. London. 1827

COVENTRY (Thomas.) Treatise on the Stamp Laws. 8vo. 3,50. London. 1833

COVENTRY (Thomas.) On Conveyancer's Evidence. 8vo. 1,75. Philadelphia. 1839

COVENTRY (Thomas.) A Readable edition of Coke upon Littleton. 8vo. 2,25. London. 1830
(Published at 16s. *bds.*)

COWEN (Esek.) Reports of Cases in the Supreme Court and Court of Errors, in New York, from 1823 to 1829. 9 vols. 8vo. 6,00 a volume. Albany. 1824–30

COWEN (Esek.) Treatise on the Civil Jurisprudence of Justices of the Peace. 3d edition. By O. L. Barbour, Counsellor at Law. 2 vols. 8vo. 7,00. Albany and New York. 1844

COWPER (Henry.) Reports of Cases in King's Bench, from Hil. 14 Geo. III. 1774, to Trin. 18 Geo. III. 1778. 1st Am. ed., with Notes, &c. 2 vols. 8vo. 5,00. Boston. 1809

COWPER (Henry.) The same. 2 vols in 1. 3,50. New York. 1833

COWPER (Henry.) The same, (condensed) in 1 vol. 4,00. Secondhand. London. 1800

COX (Samuel Crompton.) Cases determined in the Courts of Equity, from 1783 to 1796 inclusive, with a few of an earlier date. By Lord Hardwicke, and Lord Northington. 2 vols. 8vo. 7,50. London. 1816

Coxe (Richard S.) Reports of Cases in the Supreme Court of New Jersey, from 1790 to 1795. Vol. I. 8vo. 3,00. Burlington, N. J. 1816

Crabbe (George.) History of the English Law, from the earliest period. 1st Am. ed. 8vo. 3,50. Burlington. 1831

Crabbe (George.) Digest and Index, with a Chronological Table of all the Statutes from Magna Charta to 1841. 8vo. 9,00. London. 1841

Cragii (D. Thomæ.) Jus Feudale, editio tertia, edidit J. Baillie. Folio. *old cf.* 4,50. Edinburgh. 1732

Cranch (William.) Reports of Cases in the Supreme Court of the United States, from August, 1810, to February, 1815. 9 vols. 18,00. Washington. 1817

Criminal Code. Burglary, House-breaking, and Church-robbing. Folio. *half bd.* 2,00. London. 1826

Criminal Code. Forgery. Folio. *half bd.* 3,50. London. 1826

Criminal Code. Coining. Folio. *half bd.* 2,00. London. 1825

Croke (Sir George.) Reports of Cases in King's Bench and Common Pleas, in the Reigns of Elizabeth, James I. and Charles I. Revised by Sir Harbottle Grimston. 5th ed., with Notes, &c., by Thomas Leach, Esq. 8vo. 3 vols. 12,00. London. 1791

Croke (Sir George.) Reports of Cases in King's Bench and Common Pleas, temp. Car. I. Folio. Title wanting. 3,50. London.

Crompton (George.) Rules and Cases of Practice in King's Bench and Common Pleas. 2 vols. 8vo. 1,50. London. 1783

Crompton (George.) The same, revised, corrected, and newly arranged, by B. J. Sellon. 2 vols. 3,00. New York. 1813

CROWN Cases reserved for Consideration and decided by the Twelve Judges of England, from 1799 to 1824. By William Oldnall Russell and Edward Ryan, from 1824 to 1837. By William Moody and by the Twelve Judges of Ireland, from May, 1832, to Nov. 1840, by Robert Jebb. 3 vols. 8vo. 9,00. Philadelphia. 1842

CROWN Circuit Companion. 1st Am. ed. Into which has been incorporated the Crown Circuit Assistant. 8vo. 3,00. New York. 1716

CRUISE (William.) On Fines and Recoveries. 2 vols. 8vo. 5,00. London. 1794

CRUISE (William.) Digest of the Laws of England respecting Real Property. 4th Am. ed. 6 vols. 8vo. 14,50. New York. 1834

CRUISE (William.) The same. 6 vols. 8vo. *cf.* 2d hand. 12,00. London. 1818

CRUISE (William.) Treatise on the Origin and Nature of Dignities or Titles of Honor. 8vo. *calf.* 1,25. London. 1810

CUJACII (Jacobi.) Opera Omnia. Editio nova Emendatior et Auctior; opera et cura C. A. Fabroti, I. C. Folio. 10 vols. 36,00. Paris. 1658

CUNNINGHAM (T.) New and Complete Law Dictionary, or General Abridgment of the Law. Folio. 2 vols. 5,00. London. 1794

CUNNINGHAM (T.) The Law of Bills of Exchange. 8vo. 1,00. London. 1778

CURRY (William.) Abridgment of Blackstone's Commentaries. 8vo. 2,50. London. 1809

CURTIS (George T.) Rights and Duties of Merchant Seamen according to the General Maritime Law and the Statutes of the United States. 8vo. 3,50. Boston. 1841

"Messrs. LITTLE AND BROWN — Gentlemen: I have read through with great care a large portion of a Treatise, by George T. Curtis, Esq., upon the Rights, Duties, and Obligations of the Owners, Masters, Officers, and Mariners of Ships in the Merchant Service. I think the work is written with great ability, accuracy, and learning, and if published it will constitute by far the most valuable treatise now in existence on this highly important branch of law, and will be worthy of extensive public patronage.

"I am, very truly and respectfully, yours,

"JOSEPH STORY."

CURTIS (George T.) A Digest of Cases Adjudicated in the Courts of Admiralty of the United States, and in the High Court of Admiralty in England, together with some Topics from the Works of Sir Leoline Jenkins, Judge of the Admiralty in the Reign of Charles II. With a copious Index. 8vo. 6,00. Boston. 1839

"A work, which shall embrace a full and accurate review of all the doctrines of the authorities upon the various subjects that come under the cognizance of the Admiralty Courts, must be of great value to every lawyer who is engaged in practice in any of our seaports. But it is equally important to underwriters, to ship-owners, and ship-masters, and shippers of goods, as it may afford them prompt information in their ordinary business. — Of course the value of such a book must essentially depend upon its fulness, accuracy, clearness of statement, and practical convenience of arrangement. In our judgment, Mr. Curtis's work, in all these respects, deserves the praise of being not merely good, but excellent. We cannot doubt, indeed, but that it will meet with full success. It would be an undeserved reproach to the profession, to suppose, that so useful a compendium should not at once find its appropriate place on the shelves of every commercial lawyer, who aspires to own a library."

CURTIS (George T.) The American Conveyancer, containing a large Variety of Legal Forms and Instruments adapted to popular wants and professional use. 12mo. 1,00. Boston. 1839

"Of the different books of forms and precedents, the larger works on conveyancing, prepared especially for the profession, and generally copied, with little alteration, from the English books on the same subject, are far too complicated and technical for common use — while the smaller works, intended for the use of persons not of the profession, and made to sell, have been too often carelessly prepared, and, like blind guides, have led those who trusted to them into the very difficulties they sought to escape.

"The present work does not seem liable to either of these objections. It has evidently been prepared with great care. In those parts of it of a higher and more technical character, Mr. Curtis has rejected the redundancies and verbosity of the

English precedents, while he appears to have retained all that is necessary and essential. But to these, which, under one shape or another, more or less perfect, are to be found in every book of conveyancing, he has added a great variety of useful forms for every-day use — for magistrates, sheriffs, and business men, many of which we do not remember to have seen before in any work of the kind. Such are the forms for Acknowledgment of Deeds, of Summons and Notices for the taking of Depositions — of Captions for Depositions — a great variety of forms of Returns on Writs and Executions — forms of Articles of Copartnership, of Articles for Joint Stock Companies — Letters of Credit, and forms of the different Instruments for the procuring of Letters Patent. The Appendix, also, containing the whole of the Insolvent Law of Massachusetts, with forms and directions, and an Analysis of the Statute, is a most valuable addition to the work. Believing, as we do, that the more the law is known, and its speedy and economical operation is seen, the more favor it will gain, as affording a remedy to the creditor against the fraudulent debtor, and a relief to the honest debtor from the oppressive creditor. We would have it, with the explanations and directions here given, placed in the hands of every business man; for every such man, however limited his transactions may be, 'is likely to be called to take a practical share in its actual administration upon his own affairs or those of his neighbor.' — The publishers have judiciously placed this work at the moderate price of one dollar, bringing it within the means of every business man, from the opulent merchant to the laborious mechanic."

Cushing (L. S.) Insolvent Law of Massachusetts. 2d ed., with Amendments. 12mo. 1,25. 1839

Cushing (L. S.) Practical Treatise on the Trustee Process, or Foreign Attachment, of Massachusetts and Maine; with an Appendix, containing the Statutes of Massachusetts, Connecticut, Rhode Island, New Hampshire, Vermont, and Maine, on that Subject. 8vo. 2,00. Cambridge. 1833

Cushing (L. S.) Reports of Contested Elections in the House of Representatives of the Commonwealth of Massachusetts, from 1780 to 1834 inclusive. 8vo. 1,00. Boston. 1834

See *Pothier*.

Dallas (A. J.) Reports of Cases in the Courts of the United States and Pennsylvania, before and since the Revolution. 4 vols. 8vo. 12,00. Philadelphia. 1806-7

DALLAS (George.) System of Stiles as now practised within the Kingdom of Scotland, consisting of 6 parts. 4to. 2 vols. 8,50. Edinburgh. 1774

DALRYMPLE (John.) Essay towards a General History of Feudal Property in Great Britain. 3d ed. 8vo. 1,25. London. 1758

DALTON (Michael.) The Country Justice, containing the Practice, Duty, and Power of the Justices of the Peace, as well in as out of the Sessions. Folio. 2,50. *calf.* London. 1727

DANA (James G.) Reports of Select Cases decided in the Courts of Appeals of Kentucky. 9 vols. 8vo. 45,00. Frankfort, Ky. 1836

DANIEL (Edmund R.) The Practice of the High Court of Chancery. 1st American, from the 2d London, edition. With considerable Alterations and Additions, adapting the Text to the last General Orders and the most recent Decisions of the Court. By Thomas Emerson Headlam, A. M. Barrister at Law. With Notes of American Decisions of Chancery Practice, by J. C. Perkins. 2 vols. Royal 8vo. (In press.)

"The labors of Mr. Headlam have rendered this work before one of unsurpassed excellence, the most comprehensive, safe and useful Manual of Chancery Practice that has ever appeared. The additions and alterations of Mr. Headlam have greatly increased the value of the original work. Some of these additions have been made to include the numerous Decisions in Chancery Practice, which have been made since the publication of the original work in 1840; others to meet the new English Orders in Chancery, adopted in 1841 and 1845. Many of these orders have been adopted into the Chancery Practice of the Supreme Court of the United States, and of course all of these additions thereby become valuable in this country. The subscribers have the first and only copy of this *second* edition now in this country. To obtain this at an early date they have been obliged to incur a very great expense. It was at first supposed by the subscribers, that the work might be of sufficient service in this country in its present form to justify a reprint of it directly from the English edition, but, upon consulting lawyers of eminence in whom great confidence is reposed, they have become convinced, that in consequence of the difference of practice on many points between this country and England, the work could be rendered of the greatest value to the American bar, only by the adaptation of it to American practice, by the addition of Notes and References to American Decisions on matters of Chancery Practice. They have consequently thought it advisable to employ the services of Mr. Perkins in editing the work, having the fullest confidence that his experience and faithfulness, in editing works in law and equity, and especially in editing Brown's Chancery Reports, and a number of the volumes of Sumner's edition of Vesey's Reports, will be regarded a sufficient guaranty that the requisite skill and labor will be employed on the work, and that it will thereby become as useful and indispensable in this country and to American practitioners, as it is now considered in England and to English practitioners. The work will be published in a very convenient form, and at an unusually low price. It will be issued from the press with as little delay as is consistent with a faithful and thorough examinative analysis and citation of the American authorities."

DARTMOUTH COLLEGE Case, reported by Timothy Farrar. 8vo. 2,00. Portsmouth. 1819

DARTMOUTH COLLEGE, Charter of. Hanover.

DAVIES (Sir John.) Reports of Cases in Ireland. 8vo. 2,50. Dublin. 1762

DAVIS (Daniel.) Civil and Criminal Justice. 2d ed. 8vo. 2,25. Boston. 1828

DAWSON (George.) Treatise of the Origin of Laws, and their obliging Power, as also of their great Variety. Folio. 1,75. London. 1694

DAY (Thomas.) Reports of Cases in the Supreme Court of Errors in Connecticut, from 1802 to 1810, and in the Circuit Court of the United States for the District of Connecticut, from 1807 to 1812. 5 vols. 8vo. 15,00. Hartford and New York. 1806–13

DAY (Thomas.) Reports of Cases in the Supreme Court of Errors in Connecticut. Vols. 8 to 15. 4,00 a volume.

DAY (Thomas.) Reports of Cases in the Supreme Court of Errors in Connecticut (Connecticut Reports), from 1820 to 1844. 15 vols. 8vo. 90,00. Hartford. 1820–44

DAY (Thomas.) Reports of the Supreme Court of Connecticut, from 1802 to 1810. 2 vols. 8vo. 10,00. Hartford. 1817

DAY (Thomas.) A Digest of the Reported Cases decided by the Supreme Court of Errors of the State of Connecticut, from 1786 to 1839. 8vo. 5,00. Hartford. 1840

DEACON (Edward E.) Law and Practice of Bankruptcy as altered by the New Act, with a Collection of Forms and Precedents in Bankruptcy and Practical Notes. 8vo. 2 vols. *cf.* 11,00. London. 1827

D'AGUESSEAU (M. le Chancellier.) Œuvres complétes. 14 vols. 4to. 28,00. Best ed. Paris. 1787

DEBATES of the Convention of North Carolina, called to Amend the Constitution of that State, which assembled at Raleigh, June 4, 1835. 8vo. 2,50. Raleigh. 1836

DEBATES and other Proceedings of the Virginia Convention, of June, 1788. By David Robertson. 8vo. 2,25. Richmond. 1805

DEAN (Amos.) Manual of Law for the Use of Business Men. 8vo. 1,50. Albany. 1838

DELAFONS (John.) Treatise on Naval Courts Martial. 8vo. 2,50. London. 1805

DE LOLME (J. L.) Constitution of England compared with the Rupublican Form of Government and the other Monarchies of Europe. 8vo. 2,25. London. 1809

DE LOLME (J. L.) The same, edited by T. G. Western. 8vo. 2,50. London. 1841

DELVINCOURT (M.) Cours de Code Civil. 3 vols. 4to. *half cf.* 11,00. Paris. 1834

DICKINSON (Wm.) Exposition of the Law relative to the Office of Justice of the Peace, chiefly out of Session. 3 vols. 8vo. 9,00. London. 1822

DICKINSON (Rodolphus.) Town Officer. 8vo. 1,00. Boston. 1811

DICTIONNAIRE Analytique, Historique, Etymologique, etc. de la Coutume de Normandie, par M. Houard. 4 vols. 4to. 12,00. Paris. 1780

DIGEST of the Law on Libels. 4to. 1,00. London. 1765

DIGEST of Adjudged Cases, King's Bench, from the Revolution to 1775, by a Gentleman of Lincoln's Inn, London. Folio. *cf.* 5,00. 1775

DIGEST of Cases Reported in the Constitutional Court of South Carolina. 8vo. 2,50. Charleston. 1824

DIGEST of Commercial Regulations of the Different Foreign Nations. 3 vols. 8vo. 12,50. Washington. 1833

DIGEST of Term Reports. See *Tomlins.*

DIGEST of the Laws of Mississippi, comprising all the Laws of a General Nature to 1839 inclusive. By J. Fox Alden and J. A. Van Hoesen. 8vo. 6,00. New York. 1839

DIGESTED Index to the Chancery Reports. ,75. London. 1802

DIMITRY. La Philosophie du Droit. 8vo. 1,37. Paris. 1842

DIPLOMATIC CORRESPONDENCE of the United States, from September 10, 1783, to March 4, 1789, being Supplementary to Sparks's Diplomatic Correspondence. (See *Sparks.*) 8vo. 7 vols. *half cf.* 18,00. Washington, D. C. 1838

DOBIE (Alexander.) Collection of English Styles or Forms, for the Use of the Profession of the Law in Scotland. 8vo. 1,25. London. 1824

DOCTOR and STUDENT, or Dialogues between a Doctor of Divinity and Student in the Laws of England. 16th ed. 3,50. London. 1761

DODSON (John.) Reports of Cases in the High Court of Admiralty, commencing with the Judgments of Sir Wm. Scott. 8vo. 5,00. London. 1815

DOGHERTY (Thomas.) Crown Circuit Assistant. 8vo. 3,50. Dublin. 1788

DOMAT (M.) Civil Law in its Natural Order, together with the Public Law, translated into English, by Wm. Strahan, with Remarks on some Differences between the Civil Law and the Law of England. 2 vols. Folio. 13,50. London. 1722

DOMAT (M.) Les Loix Civiles dans leur Order Naturel, le Droit Public, et Legum Delectus. Revue, corrigée et augmenteé par M. de Hericourt. Folio. *cf.* 13,50. Paris. 1777

DOMAT (M.) Les Loix Civiles, &c. the same, with Notes by M. Boucheoret, &c. Folio. 5,50. Paris. 1777

DOMAT (J.) Œuvres complètes, Ed. de M. Carré. 9 vols. 8vo. *cf.* 13,50. Paris. 1821

DOUGLASS (Sylvester, Lord Glenbernie.) The History of the Cases of Controverted Elections. 4 vols. in 2. 8vo. 5,50. London. 1802

DOUGLASS (S.) Reports in the King's Bench, in 19, 20, and 21 Geo. III. 4th ed. with Notes and Additions, by W. Frere, Esq. 2 vols. royal 8vo. 7,00. London.

DOW (P. Esq.) Reports of Cases upon Appeals and Writs of Error in the House of Lords, 1813–1818. 6 vols. 8vo. 35,00. London. 1814–19

DOW (P. Esq.) and Clark (C.) The same, continued from 1827 to 1832. 2 vols. 8vo. 10,00. London. 1832

DOWLING (James.) Statutes, comprising Public Acts, Civil and Criminal, Irish and Scotch, 2 Geo. IV., 2 and 3 Wm. IV. 3 parts. 8vo. 5,00. London. 1830–3

DU BOYS (A.) Histoire du Droit Criminelle des Peuples Ancienus. 8vo. *half cf.* 3,00. Paris. 1845

DUER (John, LL. D.) The Law and Practice of Marine Insurance deduced from a critical Examination of the Adjudged Cases, the Nature and Analogies of the Subject, and the general Usage of Commercial Nations. vol. 1. 8vo. 5,00. New York. 1845

DUPIN (M.) Requisitoires Playdoyers et Discours de Rentræ. 6 vols. 8vo. *half cf.* 13,00. Paris. 1836

DU PONCEAU (Peter S.) The Jurisdiction of the Courts of the United States, with a Sketch of the National Judiciary Powers exercised prior to the adoption of the Federal Constitution, by Thomas Sargeant; and the Author's Discourse on Legal Education. 8vo. 2,50. Philadelphia. 1824

DURNFORD (Charles) and EAST (Edward Hyde.) Reports of Cases in King's Bench, from Mich. Term, 26 Geo. III. to Trin. Term, 40 Geo. III. 4th ed. 8 vols. 8vo. 16,00. London. 1794-1802

DURNFORD (Charles) and EAST (Edward Hyde.) The same. 16,00. New York. 1824

DUTTON (Henry.) The Connecticut Digest, containing all the Decisions in the 16 first vols. Connecticut Reports. 8vo. 3,00. New Haven. 1833

DUVERGER (M. F.) Manuel Criminel des Juges de Paix. 8vo. *half cf.* 2,25. Paris. 1841

DUVERGER (M. F.) Manuel des Juges d'Instruction. 2d ed. 3 vols. 8vo. *half cf.* 7,50. Paris. 1844

DYER (Sir James.) Les Reports des Divers Select Matters et Resolutions des Reverend Judges del ley temp. Hen. VIII., Ed. VI., Mar., and Eliz. Folio. 3,50. London. 1672

DYER (Sir James.) The same, translated, with Life and References, &c. By John Valliant. 3 vols. 8vo. 9,00. London. 1794

EAGLE (Wm.) The Magistrate's Pocket Book, containing the Duties of a Justice, &c. 12mo. 2,50. London. 1839

EAST (Edward Hyde.) Reports of Cases in King's Bench, with Notes, &c. By Thomas Day. 16 vols. 8vo. 30,00. Philadelphia. 1817

EAST (Edward Hyde.) The same, with Notes, by G. M. Wharton. 16 vols. in 8. 20,00. Philadelphia. 1845

EAST (Edward Hyde.) Reports, the following odd vols.: 1, 2, 3, 4, 7, 9, 10, 12, 13, 14, 15, 16, for sale separately, at 1,00 a volume.

EAST (Edward Hyde.) A Treatise of the Pleas of the Crown. 2 vols. 5,00. Philadelphia. 1806

EDEN (Frederic.) Sketch of the International Policy of Modern Europe. 8vo. ,75. London. 1823

EDEN (Robert Henley.) Reports of Cases argued and Determined in the High Court of Chancery, from 1757 to

1766. From the Manuscripts of Lord Northington. 2 vols. in 1. 8vo. 4,50. Philadelphia. 1839

EDEN (Robert Henley.) Treatise on the Law of Injunctions. 8vo. 3,00. Albany. 1839

EDEN (William, Ld. Auckland.) Principles of Penal Law. 2d ed. 2,50. London. 1771

EDWARDS (Thomas.) Reports of Cases in the Court of Admiralty, from 1808 to 1812. 8vo. 2,75. New York. 1815

EDWARDS (Charles.) Reports of Chancery Cases decided in the first Circuit of the State of New York, 1831-1843. 3 vols. 8vo. 15,00.

EDWARDS (Charles.) Juryman's Guide. 8vo. 2,00. New York. 1831

EDWARDS (Charles.) On Receivers in Chancery, with Precedents. 8vo. 3,00. New York. 1839

ELLIOTT (Jonathan.) American Diplomatic Code, embracing the Treaties and Conventions between the United States and Foreign Powers, from 1778 to 1834. 2 vols. *cf.* 12,00. Washington. 1834

ELLIOTT (Jonathan.) Debates in the several State Conventions on the Adoption of the Federal Constitution. 4 vols. 8vo. 10,00. Washington, D. C. 1836

ELLIS (Charles.) A Treatise on the Law of Debtor and Creditor. 8vo. 3,50. London. 1822

EMERIGON (Balthazard-Marie.) Traité des Assurances et des Contrats à la Grosse. 2 vols. 4to. 3,50. Marseilles. 1783

EMERIGON (Balthazard-Marie.) Essay on Maritime Loans, translated by John E. Hall, with an Appendix. 8vo. 1,75. Baltimore. 1811

ENGLISH Liberties, containing Magna Charta, Charta de Foresta, Habeas Corpus, &c. &c. 8vo. 2,00. Providence, R. I. 1774

ENGLISH Common Law Reports, being Reports of Cases in the English Courts of Common Law, from 1813 to 1845, edited by Thomas Sergeant, and John C. Lowber, of the Philadelphia Bar. 45 vols. 8vo. 3,50 per vol. 1822–45

English Common Law. Single vols. 4,40 per vol.

English Exchequer Reports, containing the Reports of Cases decided in the Court of Exchequer, at Law and Equity, and in the Exchequer Chamber in Equity and in Error. Edited by Francis J. Troubat. 6 vols. 8vo. 12,00. Philadelphia. 1835

See *Price*, *Wightman*, and *M' Cleland*.

English Exchequer Reports, in continuation of Price, now reprinting in full, at 2,50 a volume. 4 vols. have already appeared. Philadelphia. 1845

English Pleader. 8vo. 1,00. London. 1734

English Ecclesiastical Reports, from 1809 to 1835. Edited by E. D. Ingraham. 7 vols. 3,50 per vol. Philadelphia. 1831–45

See *Philemore*, *Addams*, *Haggard*, *Furgerson*, and *Lee*.

Equity Digest. See *Barbour* and *Harrington*.

Espinasse (Isaac.) Treatise on the Law of Actions on Penal Statutes. 8vo. 1,25. New York. 1822

Espinasse (Isaac.) Practical Treatise on the Settling of Evidence for Trials at Nisi Prius. 8vo. 2,50. Philadelphia. 1822

Espinasse (Isaac.) Reports of Cases at Nisi Prius, in the Courts of King's Bench and Common Pleas, from East, Term 33 Geo. III. to Trin. Term 47 Geo. III. 1807. Day's ed. 6 vols. 8vo. 10,00. Hartford. 1808

Fairfield (John.) Reports of Cases Argued and Determined in the Supreme Court of the State of Maine. 3 vols. 8vo. 3,75 per vol. Hallowell. 1835–6

Faranacius (P.) Repertorium de Ultimis Voluntatibus, &c. Folio. 3,00. Leyden. 1644

Farrar (Timothy.) See *Dartmouth*.

Farrsley (Thomas.) Cases in King's Bench first year of

Queen Anne, Temp. Lord Chief Justice Holt. Folio. 2,50. London. 1725

FEARNE (Charles.) Posthumous Works, edited by Shadwell. 8vo. 3,50. London. 1797

FEARNE (Charles.) Copies of Opinions ascribed to eminent Counsel on the Will, which was the subject of the Case of Perrin *v*. Blake, before the Court of King's Bench in 1769. 8vo. 1,25. London. 1780

FEARNE (Charles.) Essay on the Learning of Contingent Remainders and Executory Devises, 10th edition, containing the Notes, Cases, and other Matter added to the former editions, by C. Butler. With an Original View of Executory Interests in Real and Personal Property, comprising the Points deducible from the Cases stated in the Treatise of Fearne, as well as Statements of, and the Conclusions from, Three Hundred additional Cases, together with References to numerous other Decisions, and so connected with the Text of Fearne, as to form a Body of Notes thereto. By Josiah W. Smith, B. C. L. Barrister at Law. 2 vols. royal 8vo. 7,50. London. 1844

FEDERALIST, on the New Constitution, written in 1788, by Alexander Hamilton, James Madison, and John Jay. 8vo. 2,00. Hallowell, Me. 1837

FÉREOL-RIVIÈRE, Esquisse Historique de la Législation Criminelle des Romains. 8vo. 1,50. Paris. 1844

FERGUSON (Wm. Dwyer.) Forms and Precedents of Practical Proceedings and Pleadings in the Courts of Queen's Bench, Common Pleas, in Ireland, with reference to the Practice. 8vo. 5,50. Dublin. 1845

FERRIÈRE (Claude Joseph.) Corps et Compilation de tous les Commentateurs Anciens et Modernes sur les Coutumes de Paris. 2d ed. 4 vols. Folio. 16,00. Paris. 1794

FINCH (John.) See *Precedents in Chancery*.

FITZ-HERBERT (Sir Anthony.) Natura Brevium. With a Commentary, supposed to be written by Lord Hale. 9th ed. 2 vols. 8vo. 11,00. London. 1714

FLAUST (Jean-Baptiste.) Explication de la Coutume et de la Jurisprudence de Normandie. 2 vols. Folio. *cf.* 7,50. Rouen. 1781

FONBLANQUE (John.) Treatise of Equity. 3d ed. 2 vols. 8vo. 5,00. London. 1820

FORMULAIRE de tous les Actes tant Civils que Commerciaux que l'on peut passer sous Seing Privé 8vo. 1,00. Bruxelles. 1839

FOSTER (Sir Michael.) Report of some Proceedings on the Commission for the Trial of the Rebels in 1746, and of other Crown Cases; to which are added Discourses upon a few Branches of the Crown Law. Folio. 6,00. Oxford. 1762

FOSTER (Sir Michael.) The same. 8vo. 3,50. Dublin. 1767

FOUCART (E. V.) Précis de Droit Public et Administratif suivi d'une Bibliographie indiquant les Ouvrages sur le Droit Administratif. 8vo. 2,25. Paris. 1844

FOUCHER (M. Victor.) Code Civil de l'Empire de Russie. 8vo. 2,25. Paris. 1841

FOURNEL (M.) Traité du Voisinage. 4th ed. 2 vols. 8vo. 3,75. Paris. 1834

FRAGMENT on Government, being an Examination of what is said on that Subject in Blackstone's Commentaries. 8vo. 1,00. Dublin. 1776

FREEMAN (Richard.) Reports of Cases in King's Bench and Common Pleas, from 1670 to 1704. 2d ed. With Notes, &c., by Edward Smirke; and in the High Court of Chancery from 1660 to 1706. With Notes by Hovenden. 2 vols. 8vo. 7,50. London. 1823–26

FREWIN (Richard.) Digested Index of the Laws of the Customs. 8vo. 3,00. London. 1819

GALE (C. J.) and WHATLEY (T. D.) Treatise on the Law of Easements. 8vo. 3,50. New York. 1840

GALLISET (C. M.) Corps du Droit Français, ou Recueil Complet des Lois, Decrets, Arrêts, Ordonnances, Senatus Consultus, Reglemens, Avis du Conseil D'État, Instructions Ministerielles, publiés depuis 1789 jusqu'à nos jours. 6 vols. 8vo. 27,00. Paris. 1833

GALLISON (John.) Reports of Cases in the Circuit Court of the United States for the First Circuit. 2d ed. With additional Notes and References. 2 vols. 8vo. 12,00. Boston. 1845

GAMBOA (F. X.) Commentaries on the Mining Ordinances of Spain. Translated from the Spanish, by R. Heathfield. 2 vols. 8vo. 4,50. London. 1830

GENERAL INDEX to the Common Law, or Tables of all the Cases printed in the Books of Reports. Digested under proper Heads, &c. &c. Folio. 2,25. London. 1726

GENTOO LAWS, a Code of, or Ordinations of the Pundits, from a Persian Translation made from the Original, written in the Sanscrit Language. 4to. 4,50. London. 1776

GILBERT (Sir Jeffrey, Lord Chief Baron.) Reports of Cases in Equity in the Courts of Chancery and Exchequer. Folio. 2,25. London. 1742

GILBERT (Sir Jeffrey, Lord Chief Baron.) The Law of Tenures, with an Historical Introduction on the Feudal System, and copious Notes, by Charles Walkins. 5th ed., by Robert Studley Vidal, Esq. 8vo. 2,25. London. 1824

GILBERT (Sir Jeffrey, Lord Chief Baron.) History and Practice of the Common Pleas. 8vo. 1,50. Dublin. 1792

GILBERT (Sir Jeffrey, Lord Chief Baron.) The Law of Distresses and Replevins. 8vo. 2,25. London. 1792

GILBERT (Sir Jeffrey, Lord Chief Baron.) The same. With Notes, by W. Impie. 4th ed. 8vo. 2,25. London. 1823

GILBERT (Sir Jeffrey.) Law of Devises and Wills. 8vo. 2,00. London. 1792

GILMAN (Charles.) Digest of the Decisions of the Supreme Courts of the States of Indiana and Illinois and the Circuit Court of the United States for the Seventh Circuit. 8vo. 5,00. Columbus, O. 1844

GILPIN (H. D.) Reports of the District Court United States of the Eastern District of Pennsylvania, 1828–1835. 8vo. 6,00. Philadelphia. 1837

GODOLPHIN (John.) The Orphan's Legacy, or a Testamentary Abridgment, in Three Parts: 1. Of Last Wills and Testaments; 2. Of Executors and Administrators; 3. Of Legacies and Devises. 4to. 1,00. London. 1701

GODWIN (William.) Enquiry concerning Political Justice, and its Influence on Morals and Happiness. 2 vols. 8vo. cf. 3,00. London. 1796

GOODWIN (R. M.) Trial for killing James Stoughton. 8vo. 1,50. New York. 1820

GORDON (George Lord) Trial of, for High Treason at the Bar of the Court of King's Bench. Folio. 2,00. London. 1783

GORDON (Thomas F.) Digest of the Laws of the United States. 8vo. 7,00. Philadelphia. 1844

GOTHOFREDUS (Dion.) Coutumes de Bourges, Tours, &c. &c. Folio. 2,50. Frankfort. 1598

GOTHOFREDUS (Jacobus.) Theodosiánus cum perpetuis Commentariis. Folio. 6 vols. in 3. 18,00. Leyden. 1665

GOULD (James.) Treatise on the Principles of Pleading in Civil Actions. 8vo. 5,00. New York. 1836

GOW (Niel.) Practical Treatise on the Law of Partnership. With Notes by Edward D. Ingraham. 2d Am. ed. from 2d Lond. ed. 8vo. 4,00. Philadelphia. 1837

GRAHAM (David.) Essay on New Trials. 8vo. 5,00. New York. 1834

GRAHAM (David.) Treatise on the Practice of the Supreme Court of New York. 8vo. 6,50. New York. 1832

GRAHAM (David, Jr.) Treatise on the Organization and Jurisdiction of the Courts of Law and Equity in the State of New York. 8vo. 5,00. New York. 1839

GRANT (Harding.) Chancery Questions and Answers. 12mo. 1,25. London. 1829

GRAVINA (Janius Vincentius.) Originum Juris Civilis Libri Tres et de Romano Imperio Liber Singularis. 4to. 3,50. Leipsic. 1737

GRAYDON (William.) Digest of the Laws of the United States. 2 vols. 8vo. 5,00. Harrisburgh, Penn. 1833

GRAYDON (William.) Forms of Conveyancing and of Practice. 2 vols. 8vo. Philadelphia. 1831

GREENE (Joshua.) A Digested Index of the Cases determined in the High Court of Admiralty before Sir William Scott, and contained in Reports of Robinson, Edwards and Dodson. 8vo. 1,25. London. 1818

GREENING (Henry.) A Collection of Forms of Declarations, and other Pleadings usually prepared in Attorneys' Offices. With Notes. 12mo. ,75. London. 1837

GREENLEAF (Simon.) A Treatise on the Law of Evidence. 2d ed. 2 vols. Royal 8vo. 11,00. Boston. 1844–6

"Professor Greenleaf has taken a difficult, important, and interesting branch of our law, and treated it with originality, clearness, neatness, method, completeness, and learning. His work will be the most agreeable manual for the student, introducing him to the principles of the law of evidence, at the same time that it will engage the attention of the practitioner, and render him most essential aid in the application of the rules to the affairs of actual life. It is not necessary to say, in enhancement of its merits, that it will supersede all other works on the same subject; but we should fail in justice to the learned author, and in expressing our high opinion of his work, if we did not frankly declare, after a careful examination of it, that no other work on the subject can be of equal value to the American lawyer, and that wherever, in our broad country, the common law is administered, Professor Greenleaf's Treatise on the Law of Evidence will be studied and referred to alike by the student and practitioner." *Am. Jur.*

"It is no mean honor to America that her schools of jurisprudence have produced two of the first writers and best esteemed legal authorities of this century; — the great and good man, who has just been taken from us, and his worthy and eminent associate, the Professor Greenleaf. Upon the existing Law of Contracts and the Law of Evidence, more light has shone from the new world than from all the lawyers who adorn the courts of Europe." *London Law Mag. Nov.* 1845.

Mr. Warren, in his new edition of his Law Studies, gives Mr. Greenleaf's work a decided preference to the more voluminous treatises of Starkie and Phillips, even for the English student. See *Law Studies*, pp. 755, 756.

GREENLEAF (Simon.) Reports of Cases in the Supreme

Court of Maine, from 1820 to 1831. 9 vols. 8vo. Per vol. 3,75. Hallowell and Portland. 1822–35

Greenleaf (Simon.) Digest of his Reports. 8vo. 3,00. Portland. 1835

Greenleaf (Simon.) Cases overruled and doubted. 8vo. 3,50. New York. 1840

Gresley (Richard Newcomb.) Treatise on the Law of Evidence in Courts of Equity. 8vo. 4,50. Philadelphia. 1837

Griffith (William.) Treatise on Jurisdiction, &c., of Justices of the Peace. 12mo. 1,00. Burlington, N. J. 1813

Griffith (William.) Annual Law Register of the United States, Vols. III. and IV. [*Vols.* I. *and* II. *not published.*] 8vo. 6,00. Burlington, N. J. 1822

Grimshaw (William.) Merchants' Law Book, being a Treatise on the Law of Attachment, Bailment, Bills of Exchange and Promissory Notes, &c. 12mo. 1,25. Philadelphia. 1831

Grotius (Hugo.) De Jure Belli ac Pacis ; Mare Liberum ac Libellum de Æquitate, etc., cum Notis, cura J. Barbeyrac. 8vo. 3,50. Amst. 1735

Grotius (Hugo.) Rights of War and Peace, translated from the Latin. Notes by J. Barbeyrac. Folio. 10,00. London. 1738

Grotius (Hugo.) Le Droit de la Guerre et de la Paix, trad. par J. Barbeyrac, avec des Notes. 2 vols. 4to. 6,00. Amsterdam. 1729

Grotius (Hugo.) Translated into English by William Evats, B. D. Folio. 4,00. London. 1682

Gude (R.) Practice of the Crown Side of the Court of King's Bench, and the Practice of the Sessions, the General Rules of Court, and the Statutes relating to the Practice ; with a Table of Fees and Bills of Cost ; also an Appendix of Forms and Precedents. 2 vols. Royal 8vo. 5,50. London. 1828

Guerard (A.) Essai sur l'Histoire du Droit Privé des Romains. 8vo. 2,25. Paris. 1814

HALE (Sir Matthew.) History of the Pleas of the Crown, published from his MSS. by Solomon Emlyn. 2 vols. Folio. 10,00. London. 1736

HALL (John E.) Practice and Jurisdiction of the Court of Admiralty. 8vo. 1,25. Baltimore. 1809

HALL (John E.) See *Emerigon. Maritime Loans.*

HALL (John E.) American Law Journal. 5 vols. 8vo. 7,50. Baltimore. 1808-9

HALL (John E.) Tracts on Constitutional Law, containing Mr. Livingston's Answer to Mr. Jefferson. 8vo. 2,00. Philadelphia. 1831

HALL (Jonathan Prescott.) Reports of Cases in the Superior Court of the City of New York. 2 vols. 8vo. 11,00. New York. 1831-33

HALE (Sir Matthew.) The Jurisdiction of the Lords, House of Parliament considered according to ancient Records, with an Introductory Preface by Francis Hayward, Esq. 4to. 4,50. London. 1796

HALSTED (William, Jr.) Reports of the Supreme Court of New Jersey, 1821-32. 4 vols. 8vo. 5,00. Trenton. 1821-32

HALSTED (William.) Reports of Cases in the Supreme Court of New Jersey, 1821-31. 7 vols. 8vo. 21,00. Trenton, N. J. 1821-31

HAMILTON (Alexander.) Works complete. 3 vols. 8vo. 7,50. New York. 1810

HAMMOND (Anthony.) Digested Index to the Term Reports and others. 2 vols. 8vo. 6,00. London. 1827

HAMMOND (Charles.) Cases in the Supreme Court of Ohio, In Bank, at December Term, 1837. Vol. VIII. 5,00. Columbus. 1838

HAMMOND (Charles.) See *Ohio Reports.*

HAMMOND (Elisha.) Treatise on the Law of Fire Insurance, and Insurance on Inland Waters. 8vo. 1,50. New York. 1840

HAMMOND (E.) Abridgment of the Law appertaining to the Office of Justice of the Peace. 8vo. 2,50. Brookfield. 1841

HAMMOND (Anthony.) Treatise on the Practice and Proceedings in Parliament and the Law of Elections. 8vo. ,75. London. 1825

HAMMOND (A.) A Practical Treatise on Parties to Actions. 8vo. 1,25. 1822

HANDS (William.) Solicitor's Practice on the Crown Side of the King's Bench, with an Appendix of Forms, &c. 8vo. 4,00. London. 1803

HANDS (William.) Rules in the Court of King's Bench. 8vo. 2,50. London. 1790

HANSARD (G.) Treatise on the Law relating to Aliens, and Denization and Naturalization. 8vo. 3,50. 1844

HANSARD'S Parliamentary History of England from the Norman Conquest, in 1066, to the Year 1803. 36 vols. 8vo. *Neat half Russia*. 70,00. London. 1806

HARDRES (Sir Thomas.) Reports of Cases in the Exchequer from 1655 to 1669. 2d ed. 8vo. 2,50. Dublin. 1792

HARDWICKE (Lord Chief Justice.) See *Cases*, &c.

HARE (Thomas.) Treatise on Discovery of Evidence by Bill and Answer in Equity. 8vo. 3,00. New York. 1836

HARGRAVE (Francis.) Collection of Tracts relative to the Law of England, from Manuscripts, now first edited. 8vo. 3,50. Dublin. 1787

HARGRAVE (Francis.) Juridical Arguments and Collections. 2 vols. 4to. *cf.* 7,50. London. 1797

HARGRAVE (Francis.) Jurisconsult Exercitations. 3 vols. 4to. 9,00. London. 1811

HARGRAVE (Francis.) Complete Collection of State Trials, and Proceedings for High Treason and other Crimes and Misdemeanors from the 11th year of Richard II. to the 46th of George III., with Alphabetical Tables to the whole. 11 vols. in 6. Imp. folio. *Neat half calf*. 36,00. London. 1770

HARPER. Reports of the Constitutional Court of South Carolina. 8vo. 3,00. Columbia, S. C.

HARRINGTON (Josiah.) Reports of Cases in the Supreme Court of New Jersey, from Feb. 1837, to Feb. 1842. 3 vols. 8vo. 10,50. Camden, N. J. 1839–42

HARRIS (Thomas,) and M'HENRY (John.) Reports of Cases in the Provincial Court, General Court, and Court of Appeals of Maryland, from 1700 to 1799. 4 vols. 8vo. Per vol. 3,50. New York. 1809–18

HARRISON (S. B.) Digest of all the Reported Cases in the House of Lords and the Courts of Common Law, from Mich. Term, 1756, to Mich. Term, 1836. 3 vols. 8vo. 10,00. London. 1837

HARRISON (Joseph.) Accomplished Practiser in the Court of Chancery. 8vo. 1,00. London. 1741

HATSELL (John.) Precedents of Proceedings in the House of Commons. 4 vols. 4to. 7,50. *cf.* London. 1796

HAUTEFEUILLE (L. B.) Code Peche Maritime. 8vo. 2,25. Paris. 1844

HAUTEFEUILLE (L. B.) Législation Criminelle Maritime. 8vo. 2,25. Paris. 1839

HAWKINS (William.) Treatise of the Pleas of the Crown. Folio. 6,00. London. 1739

HAWKINS (William.) Treatise on the Pleas of the Crown, or a System of the Principal Matters relating to that Subject, digested under proper Heads, in two Books. 8th ed. With the Statutes and Cases brought down, by John Curwood. 2 vols. royal 8vo. 9,00. London. 1824

HAWKINS (William.) Abridgment of Coke. 8vo. 2,50. Dublin. 1792

HAYES (Edmund.) Digest of the Criminal Statute Law of Ireland, with Notes, &c. 2 vols. 8vo. 8,00. Dublin. 1843

HAYWOOD (John.) Reports of Cases in the Superior Courts of North Carolina from 1789 to 1798. 8vo. 2,50. Halifax. 1799

Heath (Sir Robert.) Maxims and Rules of Pleading, with Notes, &c. By T. Cunningham. 8vo. 1,00. London. 1794

Heineccius (Jo. Gottlieb.) Antiquitatum Romanarum Jurisprudentiam Illustrantium Syntagma. 8vo. 2,50. Geneva. 1768

Heineccius (Jo. Gottlieb.) Jurisprudentia Romana et Attica, &c. 3 vols. Folio. Very fine copy. *half cf.* 21,00. Leyden. 1738

Heineccius (Jo. Gottlieb.) Opera Omnia. 10 vols. 4to. *cf.* (Best edition.) 33,50. Geneva. 1771

Heineccius (Jo. Gottlieb.) Opusculorum Variorum Syllogus. 4to. 1,25. Halæ. 1735

Heineccius Jo. (Gottlieb.) Élémens de Droit Romain, traduites annotés, corrigés, par M. Ch. Giraud. Tome premier. 2,50. Paris. 1835

Heineccius (Jo. Gottlieb.) Elementa Juris Civilis. Translated by Turnbull. 2 vols. 8vo. 6,50. London. 1763

Hennequin (M.) Traité de Législation et de Jurisprudence suivant l'Ordre du Code Civil. 2 vols. 8vo. *half cf.* 4,75. Paris. 1838

Heywood (S.) Dissertation upon the Distinctions in Society and Ranks of the People under the Anglo-Saxon Governments. 8vo. 2,00. London. 1818

Highmore (A.) On Bail. 8vo. 1,25. Dublin. 1791

Highmore (A.) On Lunacy and Idiocy. 1,25. Exeter, N. H. 1822

Hilliard (Francis.) Elements of Law. 8vo. 2,50.

Hilliard (Francis.) Treatise on the Law of Sales of Personal Property. 8vo. 3,50. New York. 1841

Hill (Nicholas, Jr.) Reports of Cases in the Supreme Court of New York. 6 vols. 8vo. 33,00. New York. 1842–5

Hippolytus Conciliorum seu Responsorum in Causis Gravissimis Redditorum. Folio. 3,50. Francfort. 1519

HISTOIRE de l'Emphytéose en Droit Romain et en Droit Français par M. E. Pepin Le Halleur. 8vo. 2,25. Paris. 1843

HISTORY of the Two Acts for the Safety of his Majesty's Person and for preventing Seditious Meetings. 8vo. 2,50. London. 1796

HISTORY, The, and Antiquities of the Exchequer of the Kings of England in two Periods — from the Norman Conquest to the end of King John, and from King John to the Reign of Edward II. Folio. 6,00. London. 1711

HOBART (Sir Henry.) Rep. Temp. Eliz. et Jac. I. reviewed and corrected by Edward Chilton. 1st Am. from 5th Eng. ed. With Notes by J. M. Williams. 8vo. 3,75. Boston. 1829

HOFFMAN (Murray.) A Treatise on the Practice of the Court of Chancery, &c. 3 vols. 12,00. New York. 1843

HOFFMAN (Murray.) Office and Duties of Masters in Chancery, and Practice in the Master's Office; with an Appenpendix of Precedents. 8vo. 3,50. New York. 1824

HOFFMAN (Murray.) Reports of Cases argued and determined in the Court of Chancery of the State of New York, before the Assistant Vice-Chancellor of the First Circuit. Vol. I. 8vo. 6,00. New York. 1841

HOFFMAN (David.) Course of Legal Study. 2 vols. 8vo. 6,00. Baltimore. 1836

HOFFMAN (David.) Legal Outlines. 8vo. 3,00. Baltimore. 1829

HOLMAN (James T.) Digest of the Reported Cases in the Courts of Tennessee from 1796 to 1835. 8vo. 5,00. Nashville. 1835

HOLMES (John.) The Statesman, or Principles of Legislation and Law. 8vo. 4,50. Augusta. 1840

HOLT (Francis Ludlow.) Law of Libel, in which is contained a General History of the Law in the Ancient Codes and of its Introduction and Successive Alterations in the Law of England. 2d ed. 8vo. 2,50. New York. 1818

HOLT (Sir John.) Reports from 1688 to 1710. Folio. 4,00. London. 1838

HOPKINS (Samuel M.) Reports of Cases in the Court of Chancery in New York. 8vo. 6,00. New York. 1827

HOPPIUS, Commentatio Succincta ad Institutiones Justinianeas &c. 4to. 3,00. Frankfort. 1731

HORSMAN (William.) Conveyancing. 3 vols. 8vo. 9,00. London. 1785

HOUARD (M.) Anciens Loix des Français, ou Additions aux Remarques sur les Coutumes Anglaises. 2 vols. 4to. 5,00. Rouen. 1779

HOUARD (M.) Traités sur les Coutumes Anglo-Normands qui ont été publiées en Angleterre depuis 11e jusqu' au 14e Siècle. 4 vols. 4to. 12,00. Paris. 1776

HOUARD (M.) See *Dictionnaire Analytique*, &c.

HOVENDEN (J. E.) General Treatise on the Principles and Practice by which Courts of Equity are guided as to the Prevention or Remedial Correction of Fraud; with numerous Incidental Notices of Collateral Points, both at Law and Equity. 2 vols. royal 8vo. 7,50. London. 1825

HOVENDEN (J. E.) Supplement to Vesey, Jun. Reports of Cases in Chancery, containing Notes, occasionally illustrated by Cases decided by Lords Hardwicke, King, &c., from the MSS. of Mr. Forrester. 2 vols. royal 8vo. 11,00. London. 1827

HOWARD (Benjamin C.) Reports of Cases in the Supreme Court of the United States. 1843-5. 8vo. 13,00. Philadelphia. 1843-5

HOWE (Samuel.) Practice in Civil Actions and Proceedings at Law in Massachusetts. 8vo. 4,50. Boston. 1834

"To students and the younger part of the profession this work will be very acceptable. And the older members, though enured by the business of their lives to the forms and points of practice, will, nevertheless, find it, not unfrequently, a useful assistant, since the memory is often treacherous, and no man's experience is so universal, as not sometimes to meet cases, such as he has never before handled. As a first attempt to settle our practice — to present it in an intelligible and systematic shape — to consolidate, as it were, and arrange the numerous regulations scattered up and down our statute book, interlacing and illustrating them by the decisions in our reports, and by the unrecorded customs and habits of the profession and of the courts, it is to be regarded with especial favor."—*Am. Jour.*

Howe (Samuel.) See *Campbell.*

Huber (U.) Prelectiones Juris Civilis secundum Institutiones et Digesta Justiniana. 3 vols. 4to. *cf.* 9,00. Loraine. 1766

Hughes (David.) Treatise on the Law of Insurance. 1st Am. ed. 8vo. 3,00. New York. 1833

Hughes (Edward.) Equity Draftsman, being a Collection of Forms of Pleadings in Equity, from the 2d London ed. 8vo. 5,00. New York. 1837

Hughes (Samuel.) See *Coventry.*

Hughes (William.) Grand Abridgment of the Law continued, or a Collection of the principal Cases and Points of Common Law from 1st Eliz. to the present time. 4to. 3 vols. 9,00. London. 1660

Hugo (Gustave.) Histoire du Droit Romain, traduite de l'Allemand par Jourdan. 8vo. 2,25. Bruxelles. 1840

Hull (William General.) Report of his Trial, by Lieut. Col. Forbes. 8vo. ,75. New York. 1814

Hume (J. D.) Laws of the Customs. 8vo. 3,50. London. 1826

Humphreys (West H.) Reports of Cases in the Supreme Court of Tennessee, 1839–44. 8vo. 4 vols. 14,00. Nashville, Tenn. 1839–44

Humphreys (James.) Observations on the Actual State of the English Laws of Real Property. 2d ed. 8vo. 1,75. London. 1827

Hutton (Sir Richard.) Rep. Temp. Jac. 1, et Car. I. Folio. 2,25. London. 1656

Ilderton (John.) Treatise or Compendium of the Law of Marine Insurance. 12mo. 1,00. New York. 1801

Impey (John.) The New Instructor Clericalis, stating the Authority, Jurisdiction, and Modern Practice of the Court of Common Pleas. 7th ed. 8vo. 3,00. 850 pp. London. 1826

IMPEY (John.) Practice of the Office of Sheriff and Under-Sheriff; also the Practice of the Office of Coroner, newly arranged and corrected. By Henry Jeremy, Esq. 8vo. 3,00. London. 1835

IMPEY (John.) Modern Practice of King's Bench. 10th ed. 8vo. 3,00. London. 1823

IMPEY (John.) The Modern Pleader. 8vo. 2,00. Dublin. 1795

INGERSOLL (Edward.) Abridgment of the Acts of Congress now in force. 8vo. 3,00. Philadelphia. 1825

INGERSOLL (J. R.) See *Roccus.*

INGRAHAM (Edward D.) View of the Insolvent Laws of Pennsylvania. 2d. ed. 8vo. 3,00. Philadelphia. 1827

INGRAHAM (Edward D.) See *Chitty*, *Condensed Chancery and Ecclesiastical Reports*, *Gow.*

INSTRUCTOR Clericalis, directing Clerks in the present Practice of the Courts of King's Bench and Common Pleas. By R. G. [R. Gardner.] 7 vols. 8vo. 11,00. London. 1614–27

IREDELL (James.) Digest of all the Reported Cases determined in the Courts of North Carolina, from 1778 to 1837, inclusive. 2 vols. 8vo. 10,00. Raleigh. 1839

IRISH Term Reports. By Ridgeway, Lapp and Schoales. 8vo. 4,50. Dublin. 1799

IRVING (David.) An Introduction to the Study of the Civil Law. 4th ed. 8vo. 2,00. London 1837

JACKSON (Charles.) Treatise on the Pleadings and Practice in Real Actions, with Precedents of Pleadings. 8vo. 3,50. Boston. 1828

"This elaborate treatise on real actions is worthy of the careful study of all who have any concern in conducting them. It has been composed with care. The learned author has given abundant evidence that he has been conversant with writings that to most lawyers are hidden mysteries. No treatise, ancient or modern, appears to have escaped his perusal.

Mistakes, not a few, he has detected and exposed. This treatise is a very complete and luminous exposition of the law of real actions, as it was when in full vigor at the close of the reign of Edward III., adapted, as the learned author supposes, to the practice in Massachusetts. It is professedly a treatise adapted to that commonwealth; and although a great part of it is of a general nature, and may be extensively useful elsewhere, yet is peculiarly applicable to Massachusetts, and as such will be considered in our remarks upon it. If the author is correct in his positions, and all that he has delivered is law in that state, it is certain that this work is indispensable for all lawyers, and, may we not add, for most judges? Many of the precedents given could be found in but very few libraries." —*Am. Jur.*

Jacob (Edward) and Walker (John.) Reports of Cases in Chancery Temp. Eldon, from 59 Geo. III. 1819, to 1 Geo. IV. 1820. 8vo. 4,00. New York. 1822

Jacob (Giles.) Law Dictionary, enlarged by Tomlins. 6 vols. 8vo. 7,50. New York. 1811

Jacob (Giles.) Statute Law. 8vo. 2,00. London. 1748

Jacob (Giles.) Treatise of Law. 8vo. 1,50. London. 1721

Jacobson (F. I.) Laws of the Sea in Peace and War. From the German, by W. Frick. 8vo. 3,50. Baltimore. 1818

Jarman (T.) A Treatise on Wills, with a copious Dissertation on the Construction of Devises; with Notes and References to American Law, by J. C. Perkins, Esq. 2 vols. 8vo. 7,50. Boston. 1845

"Cambridge, December 12, 1845.

"Messrs. Little and Brown, — I have long been acquainted with the great merit of Mr. Jarman as a legal author, and regard this treatise as one of the highest order. An American lawyer cannot well dispense with it, even in the English edition; but the notes of Mr. Perkins, who has selected the American cases with his usual skill and discrimination, have rendered the work doubly valuable to the profession.

"With much respect,

"Your obliged and obedient servant,

"S. Greenleaf."

"To Messrs. Little and Brown: Gentlemen, — I have thoroughly examined the edition of Jarman on Wills, edited by Mr. Perkins, and published by you, of which you ask my opinion. I do not hesitate to say, that it is incomparably the ablest, most complete, and best work extant upon the subject. It is no easy task, in any hands, to analyze, expound and systematize a branch of the law, having so many anomalies and perplexing difficulties, and in its nature, admitting such metaphysical subtleties, and nice and shadowy distinctions. And if Mr. Jarman's treatise is not above the reach of criticism, it is no mean praise to say, that it is far more useful for the instruction of the student and for the assistance of the practitioner, than all the books on wills which have preceded it. Mr. Jarman, indeed, seems to have been particularly well qualified, for the undertaking. He has long been advantageously known as the author of annotations, and a most able Supplement to Powell on Devises, and also as the author of copious, erudite, and practically useful notes and additions to Bytherwood's Precedents in Conveyancing. The better part of his former labors, so far as they relate to the subject, much matured and improved, of course, by reflection, and the suggestions of a considerable professional practice, is incorporated in the present treatise. It is one of the excellences of the work, that it is not, like most modern text-books, a mere agglomeration of cases under appropriate chapters and heads, with an enunciation of the doctrines, whether consistent or inconsistent, which they contain. The author canvasses, explains and criticises, with great freedom, acumen, learning and ability, the intricate, obscure, doubtful, anomalous and conflicting, as well as other cases, and enucleates therefrom the principles and real essence of the law. In the notes of Mr. Perkins, there appears to be contained, not only what is valuable in the American cases, but large quotations from, and frequent references to many English cases and authorities, unnoticed in the original text. On the whole, this edition of the work will afford very great aid in investigating difficult questions, which are constantly arising in practice, under testamentary instruments; and, I am sure, no lawyer of any considerable practice, will fail to find it highly serviceable, if not indispensable, for daily convenient reference, in matters of testamentary law.

"Respectfully yours, &c., B. RAND.

"Boston, Dec. 22, 1845."

"The work enjoys a high reputation in England; it fills up a large space, which has been long unoccupied, and we think the publishers have done an acceptable service in getting out an American edition, under the supervision of the able editor, who has bestowed much labor upon it, both in exploring and in citing the American decisions. Mr. Perkins is so well known as a careful and learned annotator, that it was scarcely necessary for him to state in the preface that 'nothing has been left undone which the editor has supposed to be necessary to render the work useful and acceptable to the legal profession in this country.' It is handsomely printed in two volumes of about eight hundred pages each." — *Law Reporter.*

JEBB (Robert.) See *Crown Cases.*

JEBB (Robert.) Cases relating to the Criminal and Presentment Law, reserved for Consideration, and decided by the Twelve Judges of Ireland, from May, 1822, to November, 1840. First American edition, with References, by John William Wallace. See *English Criminal Cases.*

JEREMY (George.) Treatise on the Equity Jurisdiction of the Court of Chancery. 1st Am. ed. 8vo. 3,50. Philadelphia. 1840

JEREMY (Henry.) Law of Carriers. 8vo. 1,00.

JEREMY (Henry.) Analytical Digest of all the Reports of Cases decided in the Courts of King's Bench, Common Pleas and Exchequer, in Chancery, at the Rolls, and in the Vice-Chancellor's Court; in Parliament, in the Consistory Court, Arches Court, Prerogative, and Peculiars, and in Bankruptcy, Nisi Prius, Crown Cases, Privy Council Cases, and Bail Court, *continued annually*, from 1824 to 1843. 21 parts, published at 9*s.* each. 8vo. 25,00. London.

JICKLING (H.) Practical Treatise on the Analogy between Legal and Equitable Estates and Modes of Alienation. Royal 8vo. 2,50. London. 1829

JOHNSON (J. E.) Analytical Abridgment of Kent's Commentaries on American Law. 8vo. 2,75. New York. 1839

JOHNSON (William.) Reports of Cases in the Supreme Court and Court of Errors of New York, from 1806 to 1823. 20 vols. 8vo. 80,00 Philadelphia. 1845

JOHNSON (William.) The same. Vols. 1, 2, 3, 4, 5, 6, separately. Per vol. 3,50.

JOHNSON (William.) . The same, in the Court of Chancery of New York, from 1814 to 1823. 7 vols. 8vo. 45,00. Philadelphia. 1836

JOHNSON (William.) Digest of Cases in the Supreme Court, the Court of Chancery, and the Court of Errors of New York, from 1799 to 1836. 3 vols. in 2. 8vo. 12,00. Philadelphia. 1838

JONES (F. C.) Attorney and Solicitor's Pocket-Book, by John Crisp, Esq. 7th ed. 2 vols. 12mo. 5,50. London. 1841

JONES (Sir William.) On the Law of Bailments. 4th ed., with Notes and References on the Subject of Carriers, Innkeepers, Warehousemen, and other Bailees, and an Essay on the Law of Coach Proprietors and Carriers. By W. Theobald. 8vo. 1,25. London. 1834

JONES (Sir William.) The Speeches of Isaeus in Causes concerning the Law of Succession to Property in Athens. 4to. 3,00. London. 1779

JONES (Sir Thomas.) Reports of several Special Cases adjudged in the Courts of King's Bench at Westminster, in the Reign of Charles II. Folio. 3,00. London. 1729

JOURNAL of the Convention for framing a Constitution of Government for Massachusetts from the Commencement of their First Session, Sept. 1, 1779, to the close of their Last Session, June 16, 1780, including a List of Members. Published by order of the Legislature. 8vo. 1,25. Boston. 1832

JOURNAL of Law. By an Association of Members of the Bar. 1,50. Philadelphia. 1831

JOURNALS of the Provincial Congress of Massachusetts in 1774-5, and of the Committee of Safety, with Appendix, &c. Published by direction of the Legislature, under the Supervision of William Lincoln. 8vo. pp. 778. 2,75. Boston. 1838

JOYNES (William I.) An Essay on the Act of the Assembly of Virginia amending the Statute of Limitations. 8vo. 2,50. Richmond, Va. 1844

JUDICIAL Chronicle, being a List of the Judges of the Courts of Common Law in Chancery, in England and America; and of the Contemporary Reports, from the earliest Period of the Reports to the present Time. 8vo. ,62. Cambridge. 1834

JUDICIARY, Debates in the Senate of the United States on the. 8vo. 2,50. Philadelphia. 1802

JURISPRUDENCE, Elements of, treated of in the Preliminary Part of a Course of Lectures on the Laws of England, by Woodeson. 4to. 2,00. London. 1783

JURIST, American. See *American.*

JUSTINIANUS (Imperator.) Pandectæ Justinianeæ, in Novum Ordinem Digestæ, cum Legibus Codicis et Novellis. Ed. J. R. Pothier. Folio. 3 vols. 30,00. Leyden. 1782

JUSTINIANUS (Imperator.) Institutionum Libri IV. cum Comment. et Notis Jani a Costa, Theodori Marcelii, et M. Antonii Mureti, curante Jo. Vande Water. 4to. 2,50. Traject. Batav. 1714

JUSTINIEN, Pandectes de, mises dans un Nouvel Ordre, par R. J. Pothier, traduites par M. de Breard Neuville. 24 vols. 8vo. 30,00. Paris. 1818

JUSTINIEN (l'Empéreur.) Institutes de, par M. Blondeau. 2 vols. 8vo. 3,75. Paris. 1836

JUSTINIEN, The Institutes of, with Notes, by Thomas Cooper, Esq. 2,00. Philadelphia. 1812

KAMES (Lord.) Historical Law Tracts. 2 vols. 8vo. 3,00. Edinburgh. 1758

KEATING (Thomas.) A Short Treatise on Family Settlements and Devises. 8vo. 1,25. London. 1810

KELHAM (Robert.) Dictionary of the Norman French Language, to which are added the Laws of William the Conqueror. 8vo. *cf.* 3,75. London. 1779

KELHAM (Robert.) Dictionary of the Roman or old French Language, collected from Acts of Parliament, old Reports and Records, &c. 8vo. 1,00. Philadelphia. 1843

KELYNG (Sir John.) Reports of Cases in Pleas of the Crown temp. Car. II. Folio. 3,50. London. 1708

KELYNG (Sir John.) The same. With Notes, by G. I. Browne. 8vo. 1,50. Dublin. 1789

KENNEDY (Vans.) Practical Remarks on General Courts Martial. 12mo. 1,62. London. 1825

KENT (James.) Commentaries on American Law. 4 vols. 8vo. 5th ed. 14,00. New York. 1844

KILTY (John.) The Landholder's Assistant and Land Office Guide. 8vo. 1,00. Baltimore. 1809

KINNE (Asa.) The most important Part of Blackstone's Commentaries reduced to Question and Answer. 3d ed. 8vo. 2,50. New York. 1842

KINNE (Asa.) Law Compendium. 4 vols. 8vo. 14,00. New York. 1844

KIRBY (Ephraim.) Reports of Cases in the Supreme Court of Connecticut, 1785–88. 8vo. 3,00. Litchfield, Ct. 1789

KITCHEN (John.) Jurisdictions; or the Lawful Authority of Courts Leet, Courts Berrin, Court of Marshalsey, &c. Edited by R. Antrobus and T. Impey. 8vo. 1,25. London. 1675

KLIMRATH (Henry.) Travaux sur l'Histoire du Droit Français Recueillis, etc. Par M. L. A. Warnkœnig. 2 vols. 8vo. 4,50. Paris. 1843

KNAPP (J. W.) Reports of Cases argued and determined before the Committees of His Majesty's Most Honorable Privy Council, appointed to hear Appeals and Petitions. 3 vols. Royal 8vo. 13,50. London. 1831–36

KNAPP (J. W.) and OMBLER (Edward.) Cases of Controverted Elections in the Twelfth Parliament of the United Kingdom. 8vo. 5,50. London. 1837

KYD (Stewart.) Treatise on the Law of Bills of Exchange and Promissory Notes. 3d ed. 8vo. 1,50. London. 1795

LAMBERT (Eli.) Treatise on Dower. 8vo. 1,00. New York. 1834

LAMBERT'S REPORTS. See *Cary.*

LANE (Richard.) Reports in the Court of Exchequer in the Time of James, being the first Collection of Exchequer Reports. Folio. 2,00. London. 1657

LANE (Thomas.) The Student's Guide through Lincoln's Inn, containing an Account of that Honorable Society. 12mo. 1,75. London. 1805

LANGDALE (Favard de.) Répertoire de la Nouvelle Législation Civile, Commerciale et Administrative. 5 vols. 4to. 21,00. 1823

LATCH (John.) Cases in the Court of King's Bench in the first three Years of the Reign of King Charles I. Folio. 2,50. London. 1720

LAW (The) of Landlord and Tenant in Ireland, by a Barrister. 8vo. 4,50. Dublin. 1841

LAW of Forfeiture for High Treason. 8vo. 1,00. London. 1775

LAW of Attorneys and Solicitors. 8vo. ,75. London. 1764

LAW of Easements. See *Gale*, &c.

LAW Tracts. 8vo. 1,25. London.

LAW Quibbles. 1,25. London. 1736

LAW, The Study and Practice of, considered in their Relations to Society. By a Member of Lincoln's Inn. 8vo. 2,00. Portland. 1806

LAW. See *Connecticut*, *Maine*, *Massachusetts*, *New York*, *Pennsylvania*, *United States*, &c.

LAW and Practice of Ejectment. 12mo. 1,00. London. 1741

LAW of Commons and Commoners. 8vo. 2,50 Lond. 1720

LAW Reporter (The) edited by P. W. Chandler. Vols. I.–VI. 8vo. 21,00. Boston. 1839–44

LAW Selections. See *Bird.*

LAWES (E.) Elementary Treatises on Pleading in Civil Actions. 8vo. 1,50. Portsmouth. 1808

LAWES (Edward.) Practical Treatise on Charter Parties. 8vo. 3,00. London. 1813

LAWS relating to Lands in the State of Ohio. 8vo. 3,00. Columbus. 1825

LAWS of the Commonwealth of Pennsylvania, from 1700 to 1844. 9 vols. 8vo. 27,00. Philadelphia. 1810–44

LAWS of England concerning Juries, by Nisi Prius, &c. 1,00. London. 1702

LAWS, Opinions and Instructions respecting the Public Lands. 8vo. 2 vols. 10,00. Washington. 1838

LAWS, Public, of Rhode Island, enacted in 1798. 8vo. 2,00. Providence. 1798

LAWS of the Commonwealth of Massachusetts, from May, 1796, to June, 1799. Vol. III. Folio. ,75. Boston.

LAWS, Perpetual, of the Commonwealth of Massachusetts from the Commencement of the Constitution, in October, 1780, to May, 1789, &c. Folio. 2,50. Boston. 1789

LAWS of the Leeward (Charibbee) Islands, from 1690 to 1730. Folio. 2,50. London. 1734

LAWS of the United States. The Public Statutes at Large of the United States of America, from the Organization of the Government, in 1789, to March 3, 1845; arranged in Chronological Order. With References to the Matter of each Act and to the subsequent Acts on the same Subject, and copious Notes of the Decisions of the Courts of the United States construing those Acts, and upon the Subjects of the Laws. With an Index to the Contents of each Volume, and a full, general Index to the whole Work, in the concluding Volume. Together with the Declaration of Independence, the Articles of Confederation, and the Constitution of the United States; and also Tables in the last Volume, containing Lists of the Acts relating to the Judiciary, Imposts and Tonnage, the Public Lands, etc. Edited by Richard Peters, Esq. Counsellor at Law. 5 vols. Royal 8vo. Boston. 1845

This first complete edition of the Laws of the United States is published in conformity with a plan proposed by the Hon. Judge Story, and approved by the Joint Committee on the Library in their report made to both Houses of Congress.

The publishers would call the attention of all those who have occasion to consult the laws of the United States to the following characteristics of this edition, which justify them in unhesitatingly recommending it as worthy of public approbation, in addition to the high testimonials in the accompanying letters as to its merits.

1. It has the sanction of Congress, and is issued under their auspices. It is to be the edition supplied to the officers of government, and an interest in the copyright is reserved to the United States.

2. It will contain *all* the laws, and yet will be put at a less price than those editions which contain only a portion of those laws. The purchaser will be sure that he can find every law which he may have occasion to refer to.

3. It is enriched with copious notes of the decisions of the courts of the United States on the several statutes, and with references to other statutes.

4. It will be the only edition in which the laws are chaptered, as is directed by the joint resolution of Congress of March 3, 1845, except the session acts, which are too expensive to be within the reach of but very few persons.

5. It can be relied upon for accuracy. It is printed with great care, from authorized editions of the laws, and then is subjected to a careful revision by the records at the seat of government. The value given to it, by so great care to secure its entire authenticity, will be at once perceived by all professional persons. The publishers would refer those whose pursuits have not given them occasion to appreciate the importance of the entire accuracy of the text to the letters of the Hon. Rufus Choate, and of the Hon. Robert C. Winthrop, which are printed herewith.

6. The superiority of the paper on which it is printed, and of its typographical execution, over all other editions, will be seen and appreciated at once by every one.

Letter from the Hon. Rufus Choate, of Massachusetts.

"Boston, December 1, 1845.

"Gentlemen, — I have examined, with some attention, the first three volumes of your new edition of the Laws and Treaties of the United States. Judging from so ample a specimen of the whole work, I can have no doubt that it will be at once and universally, and permanently, approved by the profession of law, and the country, and answer all the expectations which induced Congress to encourage and adopt it in advance. Completed as it is begun, it will contain the entire series of General and Private Laws and Resolves, obsolete or in force, chronologically arranged; all Treaties with foreign nations or Indian tribes, in the same arrangement; the Articles of Confederation and the Constitution; references, in proper places, to the decisions of all the Federal Courts applicable to any law, resolve, or treaty; and references, also, in proper places, to other laws, resolves, or treaties, upon the same subjects with those in the text. The whole succession of laws is most conveniently distributed into statutes and chapters, with a running title at the head of each page, expressing the session of Congress, and the date and chapter of each law or resolve which is contained on the page, with a full alphabetical verbal general Index of matters, and a separate Index to each volume.

"It adds, I think, greatly to the value of this edition, that you have caused every law, resolve, and treaty, to be carefully collated with the originals in the Department of State. It is thus rendered, in the most absolute sense, a standard and authoritative work; and, published as it is under the sanction of

Congress, and in obedience to a general professional and public demand, it cannot fail to supersede all other editions.

"I am your obedient servant,

"RUFUS CHOATE.

"Messrs. Little and Brown."

Letter from Hon. Robert C. Winthrop, of Massachusetts.

"Boston, November 25, 1845.

"Gentlemen, — I take pleasure in putting on paper, agreeably to your request, the favorable opinions I have already expressed, in relation to your new edition of the Laws of the United States.

"The mere fact, that your edition has been freshly and carefully compared with the originals in the Department of State, would seem sufficient commendation of it to all who appreciate the importance of an accurate text to the just understanding of the statutes. This comparison, I learn, has not been instituted in the preparation of previous editions of the laws, (except that of Bioren and Duane,) and has resulted, in the present instance, in the discovery and correction of numerous errors.

"But your edition promises to be as comprehensive and complete as it is accurate. It embraces *all the laws* which have been enacted since the foundation of our government, Private as well as Public, District as well as National, the obsolete and repealed as well as those now in force. It includes, also, all our Treaties with foreign governments and with the Indian tribes. And you have furnished it, still further, with copious references to the Decisions of the Federal Courts, and with an ample and elaborate Index. There would thus seem nothing left to be desired for the completeness of our National Code.

"I say nothing of the typographical execution of the volumes, or of the moderate price at which you propose to supply them. These matters will speak for themselves, and will combine with the other considerations which I have suggested in securing for your work the patronage it deserves. It will afford additional satisfaction to purchasers, to know that you intend to publish an annual supplement, containing the laws which may be passed by Congress from year to year, and conforming in all respects to the body of the work.

"Wishing you all success in your undertaking,

"I am, very respectfully,

"Your obedient servant,

"ROBERT C. WINTHROP.

"Messrs. Little and Brown."

Message from the President of the United States, transmitting a Communication of the Attorney General relative to a contract with Messrs. Little & Brown for certain copies of the Laws and Treaties of the United States, in pursuance of a joint resolution of the House of Representatives of March 3, 1845.

Feb. 17, 1846. *Read and referred to the Committee of Ways and Means.*

To the Senate and House of Representatives, — I herewith transmit a communication from the Attorney General, relating to a contract entered into by him with Messrs. Little & Brown for certain copies of their proposed edition of the Laws and Treaties of the United States, in pursuance of the joint resolution of 3d March, 1845.

James K. Polk.

Washington, February 16, 1846.

Attorney General's Office, February 10, 1846.

Sir, — I have the honor to communicate to you, for the information of the Senate and House of Representatives of the United States, that, in pursuance of authority vested in the Attorney General by the joint resolution of 3d March, 1845, I entered into a contract with Messrs. Little & Brown, of Boston, for one thousand copies of their proposed edition of the Laws and Treaties of the United States, and for such additional copies of the work as the government may from time to time require to be furnished.

I enclose two copies of the agreement, with the stipulation for its faithful performance. The originals have been filed with the first comptroller of the treasury.

In the execution of their work, the publishers have freely communicated with me, and have exhibited satisfactory proofs to me of their having taken great care, by comparison with the original rolls in the State Department, to insure fidelity and accuracy in their publication.

The publishers have delivered one thousand copies of the first volume, and have shipped from Boston the like number of the second volume, which may be expected every day. The other volumes will probably be delivered by the first of the month of May next. I have examined specimens of these two volumes, and they appear to me in all respects to conform to the contract, and I have given certificates to that effect.

I respectfully request that you will communicate this letter, with the copies of the contract, to the two houses of Congress, that such measures may be adopted for the distribution of these copies of the Laws and Treaties as it may be their pleasure to direct.

I also respectfully suggest, that, as I have no room attached to my office in which so large a number of volumes can be conveniently stored, it will be better for the public interest that the distribution may be made, through the State Department, of the respective volumes as they may be received from time to time.

I have the honor to be, very respectfully, sir,

Your obedient servant,

J. Y. Mason.

To the President.

Lawyer's and Magistrate's Magazine, in which is included an Account of every important Proceeding in the Courts at Westminster, during 1790 and 1791. 3 vols. 8vo. 5,00. Dublin. 1792–94

Lawyer's (The) Common-Place Book, by the late Judge Howe. With large Additions to the Index, by Mr. Marvin, Librarian of the Dane Law Library, Cambridge. 4to. 3,50. Boston. 1846

Lawyer's Guide, containing Precedents, Forms, &c. By W. W. Hening. 8vo. 2,00. New York. 1811

Laya (A.) Droit Anglais, ou Législation Anglaise sous la Forme de Codes. 2 vols. 8vo. 4,00. Paris. 1845

Layer (Christopher.) Whole Proceedings upon the Tryal and Attainder of, for High Treason. Folio. 3,75. London. 1722

Leach (Sir Thomas.) Cases in Crown Law, from the 4th Geo. II. 1730, to 40th Geo. III. 1800. 3d ed. 2 vols. 8vo. 4,50. London. 1800

Lebean (P. S.) Code des Bris et Naufrages. 8vo. 2,00. Paris. 1844

Lee (Richard.) Treatise of Captures in War. 8vo. 1,50. London. 1803

Lee (Thomas.) Dictionary of Practice in Civil Actions. 2 vols. 8vo. 10,00. London. 1825

Leigh (P. Brady.) Abridgment of the Law of Nisi Prius, with Notes and References to the American Cases decided subsequently to those referred to by Mr. Wharton's edition of Selwyn's Nisi Prius, by George Sharswood, Esq. of the Philadelphia Bar. 2 vols. 8vo. 7,00. Philadelphia. 1838

Leonard (William.) Reports of Cases in the Courts at

Westminster Temp. Eliz. and Jac. I. Published by William Hughes. 2 vols. Folio. 4,50. London. 1659

LEVINZ (Sir Creswell.) Collection of Select and Modern Entries, referring to the Cases in Levinz's Reports. Folio. 2,00. London. 1702

LEVINZ (Sir Creswell.) Les Rep. en Bank le Roy, commenant en le 12 An de Roy Car. II. et fini en le 8 An de Will. III. In French and English, by Salkeld. 2 vols. Folio. 7,50. London. 1722

LEVINZ (Sir Creswell.) The same in French. 2 vols. 4,50. London.

LEWIN (Thomas.) Practical Treatise on the Law of Trusts and Trustees. 8vo. 3,00. Philadelphia. 1839

LEWIS (Thomas.) Constitution, Jurisdiction and Practice of the Sheriffs' Courts of London. 8vo. 2,50. London. 1833.

LEY (Sir James.) Reports of Divers Resolutions in Law, arising upon Cases in the Court of Wards and other Courts at Westminster, in the Reigns of James and Charles I. Folio. 2,00. London. 1659

LIEBER (Francis.) Manual of Political Ethics, for the Use of Colleges and Students at Law. 2 vols. 8vo. 4,50. Boston. 1838–40

"I beg leave to say, without meaning any formal compliment whatever, that your Manual of Political Ethics is a profound work, full of deep reflection, solid principle, and sound and apposite illustrations. I have read it over superficially, but I have begun and have far advanced in the *study* of it with notes. I think your ethical and political principles just and admirable, and most instructive as to right, duties, property, social relations, government, sympathy, &c. &c., and I hope and intend to make myself familiar with your work as a text-book."—*James Kent.*

"The work abounds with profound views of government, which are illustrated with various learning. To me many of the thoughts are new, and as striking as they are new. If I may be allowed to judge of the whole work from this specimen, I do not hesitate to say that it constitutes one of the best theoretical treatises on the true nature and objects of government, which has been produced in modern times, containing much for instruction, much for admonition, and much for deep meditation, addressing itself to the wise and virtuous of all countries. The work has with me a still greater value, in that its aim and end are practical," &c. — *Extract from a letter of the Hon. Joseph Story.*

"They are both (the State and Absolutism) subjects of deep importance, and are treated in a new and very interesting manner. With some, not important exceptions, I am disposed to concur in the views which you take. I hope you will present the work to the public at an early day. It would be quite an acquisition to our literature, and do much to call public attention to subjects in which all have so great an interest." — *Extract from a letter of the Hon. John C. Calhoun.*

"Considering the systematic completeness with which the subject is handled, and the manner in which the accidents of things are put aside and the essentials aimed at, if not always reached, *Political Ethics* may be classed amongst the best treatises on Government since the days of *Aristotle.*" — *London Spectator, March* 23, 1839.

Lieber (Francis.) Legal and Political Hermeneutics, or Principles of Interpretation and Construction in Law and Politics, with Remarks on Precedents and Authorities. Enlarged edition. 12mo. 1,25. Boston. 1839

"I regard the Hermeneutics as a work eminently useful to our profession — not merely useful to students, but to men of long experience at the bar — as a most lucid exposition of the principles and admirable illustration of the science of interpretation and construction. It is a valuable contribution to the law. I have given the Ethics only a cursory examination in MS.; but from this rapid glance I am induced to believe, that it is well worthy the reputation of the author; and I cannot but think that the public will regard the publication as a permanent addition to the sound and useful learning of the day — destined, not like many other publications, to serve but for a day — but rather to incorporate itself into the more enduring fabric of solid science." — *Extract from a letter of Mr. Greenleaf, Professor of Law at Cambridge.*

Lilly (John.) Collection of Modern Entries, or Select Pleadings in King's Bench, Common Pleas, and Exchequer. 2 vols. 8vo. 5,00. Dublin. 1792

Lilly (John.) Practical Conveyancer, containing Rules and Instructions for drawing all sorts of Deeds for the conveying of Estates, Wills, &c. &c.; also a complete Collection of the most useful Cases in Chancery under all the Titles of Conveyancing. Folio. 3,00. London. 1742

LINDWOODE'S Provinciale. Folio. 10,00. Paris. 1501

LITTLETON'S Tenures in English. (A new edition, beautifully printed.) 12mo. 1,25. London. 1845

LITTLETON (Edward Leigneur.) Reports temp. Charles I. Folio. 3,00. London. 1683

LIVERMORE (Samuel.) Treatise on the Law of Principal and Agent, and Sales by Auction. 8vo. 1,25. Boston. 1811

LIVINGSTON (Edward.) System of Penal Law for the State of Louisiana. 8vo. 5,00. Philadelphia. 1834

LIVINGSTON (Edward.) Introductory Report to the Code of Prison Discipline. 8vo. 1,00. Philadelphia. 1827

LOCRE (M. Le Baron.) La Législation Civile, Commerciale, et Criminelle de la France, ou Commentaire et Complément des Codes Français. 16 vols. 8vo. *half calf.* 24,00. Paris. 1827

LOMAX (John T.) Treatise on the Law of Executors and Administrators generally in use in the United States, adapted more particularly to the Practice of Virginia. 8vo. 2 vols. 10,00. Philadelphia. 1841

LOMAX (John T.) Digest of the Laws of Real Property generally adopted in the United States, more especially of Virginia. 3 vols. 8vo. 14,00. Philadelphia. 1839

LONG (George.) Treatise on the Law relative to the Sales of Personal Property. With Additions, by Benjamin Rand, Esq., Counsellor at Law. 2d Am. from last Lond. ed. 8vo. 3,50. Boston. 1839

"The present volume contains ample evidence of the editor's learning and research. He is evidently thoroughly acquainted with everything relating to the subject of sales, which is of authority in the courts of England or America, and his copious additions have greatly increased the value of the original work." — *Am. Jur.*

LOUISIANA Reports, condensed. See *Condensed.*

LOVELASS (Peter.) The Law's Disposal of an Estate of a Man who dies without Will. 8vo. 2,25. Philad. 1839

LOVELASS (Peter.) The same. From the 25th London edition. 8vo. 3,00. Philadelphia. 1839

LUBÉ (D. G.) Analysis of the Principles of Equity Pleading. 8vo. 3,00. New York. 1840

LUCAS (Robert.) Cases in Law and Equity, chiefly during the Time of the Earl of Macclesfield. Folio. *cf.* 3,00. London. 1741

LUDERS (Alexander.) Tracts on Various Subjects in the Law and History of England. 2 vols. 12mo. *cf.* 4,00. London. 1810

LUTWYCHE (Edward.) Un Livre des Entries, contenant auxi un Rep. des Resolutions del Court enter le 34 Car. II. et le 2 Ann. Fr. and Lat. 2 vols. Folio. 6,00. London. 1740

LUTWYCHE (Edward.) The same. Truly stated in English. By W. Nelson. Folio. 6,75. London. 1717

MACKELDEY (Ferdinand.) Compendium of Modern Civil Law, translated by P. I. Kaufman. 8vo. Vol. I. 6,50.

MACOMB (Alexander.) The Practice of Courts Martial. 8vo. 2,00. New York. 1840

MACPHERSON (William.) Treatise on the Law relating to Infants. In Two Parts. 8vo. 8,00. London. 1841-2

MADDOCK (Henry.) Reports of Cases in the Court of the Vice-Chancellor, temp. Plumer and Leach, from 1815 to 1821. 6 vols. in 3. 8vo. 12,00. Philadelphia. 1829

MADDOCK (H.) Treatise on the Principles and Practice of the Court of Chancery, under the following heads: — 1. Common Law Jurisdiction of the Chancellor; 2. Equity Jurisdiction of the Chancellor; 3. Statutory Jurisdiction of the Chancellor; and, 4. Specially delegated Jurisdiction of the Chancellor. 3d ed., with considerable Additions. 2 vols. Royal 8vo. 7,50. London. 1837

MALLORY (John.) Modern Entries, a Select Collection of Pleadings in the Courts of King's Bench, Common Pleas, and Exchequer, &c. &c. 2 vols. 8vo. 3,00. Dublin. 1791

MAINE Reports. 22 vols. See *Greenleaf*, *Fairfield*, *Shepley*, *Appleton*.

MANNING (James.) Digest of the Nisi Prius Reports, including Peake, Espinasse, Campbell, Holt, and Starkie, and some original Cases, collected on the Western Circuit. 2d ed. 8vo. 3,75. London. 1820

MANNING (James.) The same. First American from the last London edition. 8vo. 3,00. Exeter. 1832

MANNING (James.) Notes and Proceedings of Courts of Revision, held in 1832. 12mo. 1,50. London. 1833

MANSEL (George B.) Treatise on the Law and Practice of Demurrer to Pleading and Evidence. 8vo. Philadelphia. 1839

MANSEL (George B.) Practice upon Writ of Trial for Debts not exceeding £20. 12mo. 1,50. London. 1833

MANUSCRIPTS. Pleading and Reports. 2 vols. Folio. 2,50. *vellum.*

MARCH (John.) Reports of Cases in King's Bench and Common Pleas, from 15 to 18 Car. I. 2d ed. 4to. 2,25. London. 1675

MARRIOTT (Sir James.) Formulary of Authentic Instruments, Writs, and Standing Orders used in the Admiralty, of Prize and Instance. 8vo. 1,25. London. 1802

MARSHALL (Charles.) Reports of Cases argued and determined in the Court of Common Pleas, containing Cases in 54th and 55th Year of Geo. III. 8vo. *cf.* 5,50. London. 1815

MARTENS (G. F. von.) Summary of the Law of Nations, founded on Treaties and Customs of the Modern Nations of Europe, with a List of the principal Treaties concluded since 1740 down to the present Time; translated from the French, by William Cobbett. 8vo. 2,50. Philadel. 1795

MARTIN'S Reports, Condensed. Reports of Cases in the Supreme Court of Louisiana. By H. Martin. The 20 vols. condensed. 4 vols. 8vo. 20,00. 1840

MASON (William P.) Reports of Cases in the Circuit Court of the United States for the First Circuit, from 1816 to 1830. 5 vols. 8vo. Per vol. 6,00. Boston. 1819–31

"These Reports comprise the Decisions of Mr. Justice Story

on the First Circuit of the United States, and follow in order after Mr. Gallison's Reports. The decisions relate to a great variety of subjects — Constitutional, Admiralty, Personal and Real Law, and Chancery, and are characterized by the profound learning, acuteness and thoroughness of research, which are such eminent traits of their author. They will bear a favorable comparison, in point of learning and practical utility, with the best volumes of the English Reports."

MASSACHUSETTS. General Laws, from the Adoption of the Constitution to Feb. 1822, with the Constitutions of the United States and of this Commonwealth, &c., revised by authority of the Legislature, by Asahel Stearns and Lemuel Shaw. Edited by Theron Metcalf. 2 vols. 8vo. 5,00. Boston. 1823

MASSACHUSETTS. The same, from June 1822 to June 1827, edited by Theron Metcalf, making Vol. III. 8vo. Boston. 1827

MASSACHUSETTS. Private and Special Statutes from 1780 to Feb. 1822. 5 vols. 8vo. 10,00. Boston. 1805–23

MASSACHUSETTS Reports. Tyng's Reports of Cases in the Supreme Judicial Court of Massachusetts, from 1804 to 1822. Third edition, stereotyped. With Notes, by Benjamin Rand, Counsellor at Law. Vol. I. by Ephraim Williams. 17 vols. 8vo. 62,00. Boston. 1838–40

"These Reports embrace the Decisions of the Supreme Court of Massachusetts, from the time in which they first began to be published until Mr. Pickering commenced his labors as reporter. During a portion of this period, Chief Justice Parsons, whose character for learning and ability has been so widely diffused, presided on the bench. No Reports have sustained a higher reputation throughout the country than these, or have been more extensively cited. The greater part of the present volumes have been stereotyped, and have been enriched by the learned annotations of Benjamin Rand, Esq., of the Boston bar.

MASSACHUSETTS Reports, Digest of. See *Minot.*

MATTER (M.) De l'Influence des Mœurs sur les Lois et de l'Influence des Lois sur les Mœurs. 8vo. 2,00. Paris. 1832

MATTHEWS (Richard.) Practical Guide to Executors and Administrators. 8vo. 2,00. Philadelphia. 1833

MATTHEWS (John H.) Treatise on the Doctrine of Presumption and Presumptive Evidence, as affecting the Title to Real and Personal Property; with Notes and References to American Cases, by Benjamin Rand. 8vo. 4,50. New York. 1830

MAULE (George) and SELWYN (William.) Reports of Cases in King's Bench, containing Cases of Hilary, Easter, and Trinity Terms, 1813; Michaelmas, Hilary, and Easter Terms, 1813-14, and Trin. Mich. and Hil. Terms, 1814-15. In the 53d, and 54th, and 55th Years of Geo. III. Edited by Theron Metcalf, in 2 vols. 8vo. 7,50. Condensed. Boston. 1832

"These are very valuable Reports of the Common Law in the King's Bench in England, embracing several years of the period during which those great judges, Lord Ellenborough and Sir John Bailey, were on the bench, and forming a very important link in the series of Common Law Reports. The six volumes have been condensed into two, with great skill and correctness, by Theron Metcalf, Esq., and form a very proper companion to the *English Common Law Reports*, published at Philadelphia."

MAULE (George) and SELWYN (William.) The same, *entire.* 4 vols. 8vo. 16,00. London. 1814-17

MAXWELL (John Irving.) Pocket Law Dictionary. 12mo. 1,00. *cf.* Philadelphia. 1808

MAYLNES (Gerard.) The Ancient Law Merchant. Folio. 1,50. London. 1685

MAYNZ (Charles.) Élémens de Droit Romain. 8vo. 2,25. Brussells. 1845

M'LEAN (John.) Reports of Cases argued and decided in the Circuit Court of the United States for the Seventh Circuit. Vols. I. and II. 8vo. 10,00. Cincinnati and Columbus. 1840-3

McARTHUR. The Principles and Practice of Naval Courts Martial. 8vo. 2,00. London. 1792

M'CLELAND (Thomas) and YOUNGE (Edward.) Reports of Cases in the Exchequer and Exchequer Chamber, from Hil. Term, 5 Geo. IV. to Mich. Term, 6 Geo. IV. 8vo. See *English Exchequer*.

MEAN (Car. de.) Observationes et Res Judicatæ ad Jus Civile Leodiensium Romanorum Aliarumque Gentium, Canonicum et Feudale. Folio. 8 vols. in 4. 12,00. 1740

MENOCHIUS (J.) Conciliorum. Folio. 13 vols. in 8. 26,00. Francfort. 1628

MENOCHIUS (J.) De Presumptionibus Conjecturis. Folio. 5,50. Cologne. 1684

MERLIN (M.) Recueil Alphabetique des Questions de Droit, et Répertoire Universelle et Raisonné de Jurisprudence. 26 vols. 4to. *half cf.* 80,00. Paris. 1827

MEIGS (R. J.) Reports of Cases in the Supreme Court of Tennessee. 8vo. 5,00. Nashvile. 1840

MERIVALE (J. H.) Reports of Cases in Chancery, from Mich. Term, 56 Geo. III. 1815, to Mich. Term, 57 Geo. III. 1817. 3 vols. 8vo. 8,00. New York. 1825

METCALF (Theron.) Reports of Cases argued and determined in the Supreme Judicial Court of Massachusetts. Vols. I. to VIII. 8vo. 5,00 per vol. Boston. 1840-6

Mr. Metcalf is the successor to Mr. Pickering.

METCALF (Theron.) See *Massachusetts Laws*, *Starkie*, *Yelverton*.

METCALF (Theron) and PERKINS (J. C.) and CURTIS (G. T.) Digest of the Decisions of the Courts of Common Law and Admiralty in the United States. See *United States Digest*.

MILES (John.) Reports of Cases in the District Court of the City and County of Philadelphia. 2 vols. 10,00. Philadelphia. 1836-42

MILLER (John.) Inquiry into the Present State of the Statute and Criminal Law of England. 8vo. 2,00. London. 1822

MILLER (John.) An Inquiry into the Present State of the Civil Law of England. 8vo. *cf.* 2,50. London. 1825

MILLER (John.) Historical View of the English Government, from the Settlement of the Saxons to the Revolution in 1688. 4 vols. 8vo. 10,00. London. 1803

MINOR (Henry.) Reports of Cases in the Supreme Court of Alabama. Vol. I. 1820-26. 8vo. 3,50. New York. 1839

MINOT (George.) A Complete Digest of the Massachusetts Reports, 17 vols.; Pickering's Reports, 24 vols.; and Metcalf's Reports, 4 vols. 8vo. 7,50. Boston. 1844

"I would call the attention of the profession to it, as the completest specimen of a Digest that has yet appeared. The table of cases, at the beginning, refers both to the page of the Reports and of the Digest, and there is a very full index at the end. But the greatest merit will be found in the clearness and brevity with which the points are stated. Mr. Minot appears to have examined each case for himself, and extracted the very essence of it. And although a digest is never regarded as authority, with the exception of Comyn, my examination of this induces the belief that there would be little danger in making this another exception.—*Judge Walker, in the Western Law Journal of June*, 1844.

MITFORD (John, Lord Redesdale.) Treatise on the Pleadings in the Court of Chancery. 3d Am. ed., with Notes and References, by Charles Edwards. 8vo. 3,50. New York. 1840

MODERN Entries, in English. A select Collection of Pleadings in the Courts of King's Bench, Common Pleas, and Exchequer; also all kinds of Writs, together with Readings and Observations on the several Cases in the Reports, &c. &c. 3 vols. Folio. 6,75. London. 1741

MODERN Reports; or Select Cases adjudged in the Courts of K. B., Ch., C. P., and Exc., from the Rest. of K. Ch. II. to 28th Geo. II. 5th ed. By T. Leach. 12 vols. Royal 8vo. 24,00. London. 1793-6

MOLLOT. Regles sur la Profession d'Advocat. 8vo. *half cf.* 2,50. Paris. 1842

MOLLOY (Charles.) De Jure Maritimo et Navali, or a Treatise of Affairs Maritime and of Commerce. 9th ed. 2 vols. 8vo. 6,50. London. 1769

MONTAGU (Basil.) Digest of the Law of Partnership, with a Collection of the Cases decided upon that Subject. 1st Am. ed. 2 vols. 8vo. 6,50. New York. 1832

MONTAGU (Basil.) Summary of the Law of Set-off. 8vo. 1,25. Philadelphia. 1825

MONTAGU (Basil.) Digest of the Law of Partnership. 2 vols. 8vo. 8,00. London. 1815

MONTAGU (Basil.) The same. 2 vols. 8vo. 6,50. New York. 1824

MONTAGU (Basil) and OVERTON (Scrope.) Digest of the Bankrupt Laws as altered by the New Statutes, and Practical Precedents. 3d ed., with Additions. 2 vols. 8vo. 9,00. *cf.* London. 1837

MONTEFIORE (J.) American Trader's Compendium, containing the Laws, Customs, and Regulations of the United States relative to Commerce. 8vo. 1,50. Philadelphia. 1811

MONTESQUIEU (C. de Secondat.) Œuvres Complètes avec des Notes de Dupin, Cavier, Voltaire, Mably, Servan et La Harpe. Royal 8vo. 2,25. Paris. 1838

MONTESQUIEU, Œuvres de, avec les Notes de Tous les Commentateurs, édition publiée par L. Parrelle. 8 vols. 8vo. 12,00. Paris. 1826

MOODY (William.) See *Crown Cases Reviewed*, &c.

MOORE (John Bailey.) Digested Index to the Reports of King's Bench and Common Pleas. 8vo. 2,00. London. 1825

MOORE (John Bailey.) Digested Index to the Term Reports, containing all the Points of Law argued and determined in the King's Bench and Common Pleas from 1785 to 1818, with Notes, References, and Table of Titles, continued to the present Time; by T. E. Hall. 2 vols. 8vo. 5,50. Philadelphia. 1819

MORGAN (John.) Essays upon the Law of Evidence, New Trials, Special Verdicts, Trials at Bar, and Repleaders. 3 vols. 8vo. 3,50. Dublin. 1789

MORGAN (John.) Attorney's Vade-Mecum and Client's Instructer, treating of Actions, of Prosecuting and Defending them, of the Pleadings and Law, &c., with Precedents. 3 vols. 8vo. 3,00. Dublin. 1787–8

MORIN (Achille.) Dictionnaire du Droit Criminel. Royal 8vo. 4,50. Paris. 1842

MORTON (T. C.) A Practical Treatise on the Law of Venders and Purchasers of Chattels Personal. 8vo. 3,50. London. 1837

MOSES (Myer.) Commercial Directory, and Digest of Laws of the United States relating to Commerce; including a Tariff of Rates of Duties, and Tables of Calculations applicable to all Manufactories of Wool or Cotton imported into the United States. 8vo. 2,00. New York. 1830

MOYLE (Robert.) Book of Entries of the most Select Judicial Writs used in the Common Law. 4to. 1,50. London. 1658

MUCHALL (William.) Doctor and Student, or Dialogues between a Doctor of Divinity and a Student in the Laws of England. 8vo. 1,25. Dublin. 1792

MURRAY (Sir Thomas.) The Laws and Acts of Parliament made by King James I. and his Royal Successors, Kings of Scotland. Folio. 5,50. Edinburgh. 1681

NELSON (William.) Law and Customs of England relating to Manors and Lords of Manors. Folio. 2,00. London. 1726

NEW ENGLAND Sheriff, being a Digest of the Laws of Massachusetts relating to Sheriffs, &c. 12mo. 1,50. Worcester. 1844

NEW HAMPSHIRE. Perpetual Laws, from 1776 to 1789. 8vo. 1,00. Portsmouth. 1789

NEW HAMPSHIRE Reports. Cases in the Supreme Court from 1816 to 1842. 11 vols. 8vo. Per vol. 4,00. Exeter, Concord, Chester and Newport. 1819–1842

NEWLAND (John.) A Treatise on Contracts within the Jurisdiction of Courts of Equity. 8vo. 4,00. London. 1806

NEW YORK DIGEST. See *Cambreleng*, *Clerke*.

NICHOLL (H. J.) and HARE (Thomas.) Cases relating to Railways, argued and adjudged in the Courts of Law and Equity. Vols I. and II. London. 1842–3

NORTH CAROLINA Reports. 16 vols. 8vo. Per vol. 5,00. Raleigh. For *Titles*, see *Index and Reports under the head of each State.*

NORRIS (Joseph P.) See *Peake.*

NOVELLÆ Legis Theodosii Junioris et Valentiniani III. 12mo. 2,50. 1776

NOY (Sir William.) Reports temp. Eliz., Jac. I., and Car. I. Folio. 3,50. London. 1656

NOY (William.) Grounds and Maxims with an Analysis of the Laws of England. 2d Am. from 9th Lond. ed. Edited by William Hening. 8vo. 1,50. Richmond. 1824

O'DONNEL (M.) and BRADY (Francis.) A Treatise on the Law of all Actions and Suits within the Jurisdiction of the Civil Bill Court and the Principles, Pleading and Evidence relating thereto. 8vo. 6,50. Dublin. 1844

OHIO Reports, Condensed, being Decisions in the Supreme Court of Ohio, from 1821 to 1831, reported in the four first vols. of Hammond, edited by P. B. Wilcox. 8vo. 6,50. Columbus. 1832

OHIO Reports, complete (first four vols. condensed.) 13 vols. 8vo. 39,00. 1842–45

OHIO Reports of Cases at Law and Chancery, decided by the Supreme Court during the Years 1831–1834, by John C. Wright, late Judge in said Court. 8vo. 5,00. Columbus. 1835

OHIO Reports, by Hammond. Vols. V. VI. VII. VIII. 20,00. Cincinnati. 1838

OKEY (Charles Henry.) Digest of the Law, Usage and Custom relating to the Commercial and Civil Intercourse of the Subjects of England and France. 2d ed. 8vo. 1,25. Paris. 1829

OLIVER (Benjamin Lynde.) Practical Conveyancing; a Selection of Forms of General Utility, with Notes. 3d ed. 8vo. 3,75. Hallowell, Me. 1845

OLIVER (Benjamin Lynde.) Forms of Practice, or American Precedents in Actions, Personal and Real, with Annotations. 8vo. 4,00. Boston. 1841

OLIVER (Benjamin Lynde.) American Citizen. 8vo. 2,00. Boston. 1822

OLIVER (Benjamin Lynde.) Law Summary. 2d ed. Hallowell. 1833

OLIVER (Benjamin Lynde.) Forms in Chancery, Admiralty, and at Common Law, adapted to the Practice of the Federal and State Courts. 8vo. 3,00. Boston. 1842

OLIVER (Benjamin Lynde.) See *Story*.

OPINIONS of the Attorney General of the United States from the Commencement of the Government down to the 1st of March, 1841. 8vo. 7,50. Washington. 1842

ORD (Mark.) Essay on the Law of Usury. By Thomas Day. 3d ed. 8vo. ,75. Hartford, Ct.

ORDENANZAS Generales de la Armada Naval. 2 vols. Folio. 8,00. Madrid. 1793

ORFILA (M.) Traité de Médicine Légale. 3d ed. 4 vols. 8vo. and Atlas, 4to. 10,00. Paris. 1836

ORTOLAN (M.) Cours Public d'Histoire du Droit Politique et Constitutionel. 8vo. 2,25. Paris. 1844

OSBORNE (D. G.) The Nature and Form of Actions and Rules and Principles of Pleading, in a Series of Questions and Answers. 12mo. 1,25. London. 1844

OTTO (Ed.) See *Thesaurus Juris Romani*.

OULTON (A. N.) Index to the Statutes at present in force in or affecting Ireland, from the Year 1310 to 1844. 2d ed. 2 vols. 8vo. 14,00. Dublin. 1839–45

OWEN (Samuel.) Treatise on the Law and Practice of Bankruptcy. 8vo. 3,50. New York. 1842

OWEN (Thomas.) Reports. Folio. 2,00. London. 1650

PAINE (Elijah, Jr.) Reports of Cases in the Circuit Court of the United States for the Second Circuit, from 1810 to 1826. 8vo. 5,00. New York. 1827

PAINE (Elijah) and DUER. Practice in Civil Actions and Proceedings at Law in the State of New York, in the Supreme Court and other Courts of the State, also in the Courts of the United States. 2 vols. 8vo. 5,00. New York. 1830

PALEY (William.) Treatise on the Law of Principal and Agent, with Additions by Niel Gow, and a Digest of American Decisions on this subject. 2d Am. ed. 8vo. 3,00. Exeter. 1822

PARANT (M.) Lois de la Presse en 1836, ou Législation Actuelle sur l'Imprimerie et la Librairie. 8vo. 2,25. Paris. 1836

PARDESSUS (J. M.) Collection de Lois Maritimes antérieures au XVIII.e Siècle. 5 vols. 4to. 20,00. Paris. 1828

PARDESSUS (J. M.) Traité des Servitudes ou Services Fonciers. 8vo. 1,75. Bruxelles. 1840

PARK (James Allen.) System of the Law of Marine Insurances, with three Chapters on Bottomry, on Insurances on Lives, on Insurances against Fire. 5th ed. 8vo. 3,00. Boston. 1800

PARK (John James.) Treatise on the Law of Dower; particularly with a View to the Practice of Conveyancing. 8vo. 2,00. Philadelphia. 1836

PARK (John James.) A Contre-Projet to the Humphreysian Code and to the Projets of Reduction of Messrs. Hammond, Uniacke and Twiss. 8vo. 1,25. London. 1828

PARKE and JOHNSON's Digest. A Digest of the Revised Code and Acts passed by the Legislature between the 7th day of April, 1830, and the 16th day of June, 1836, forming, with Purdon's Digest of 1830, a complete Digest of the Laws of Pennsylvania to the present Time. 2 vols. in 1. 8vo. 6,00. Philadelphia.

PARKER (Sir Thomas.) Reports of Cases concerning the Revenue, argued in the Exchequer, from East. Term, 1743, to Hil. Term, 1767. 4,50. London. 1776

PARKES (Joseph.) History of the Court of Chancery, with Practical Remarks, &c. 8vo. 4,50. London. 1828

PARLIAMENTARY Debates in the House of Commons, from 1667 to 1694. By Hon. H. Grey. 10 vols. 8vo. 12,50. *cf.*

PARLIAMENTARY History of England. See *Cobbett* and *Hansard.*

PARLIAMENTARY Journals of the House of Lords from 1509 to 1726. 22 vols. Folio. *half cf.* 26,50. London.

PARLIAMENTARY Minutes of the Committee of Council on Education, with Appendices and Plans of School-Houses. 2 parts. 4,00.

PARLIAMENTARY Reports. Reports respecting the Harbors of Holyhead and Pynllaen, with Plans. By Sir John Rennie and Mr. Page. 2 parts. Folio. 1,00. Lond. 1844

PARLIAMENTARY Reports (Bowring's) on the Commercial Relations of France and England — Silks and Wine. 2 parts. Folio. 2,50. London.

PARLIAMENTARY Reports (Bowring's) on the Manufactures, &c. of Switzerland. Folio. 1,00. London.

PARLIAMENTARY Reports (Bowring's) on the Commercial Statistics of Syria. Folio. 1,00. London.

PARLIAMENTARY Reports (Bowring's) on the Statistics of Tuscany, &c. Folio. 1,00. London.

PARLIAMENTARY Reports (Bowring's) on Egypt and Candia. Folio. 1,00. London.

PARLIAMENTARY Reports (Bowring's) on the Prussian Commercial Union. Folio. 1,00. London.

PARLIAMENTARY Reports. British Shipping. Folio. 1,00. London. 1844

PARLIAMENTARY Report, on the Census of Ireland. Folio. 2,00.

PARLIAMENTARY Report, from the Select Committee on the West India Colonies. Folio. 3,00. London. 1843

PARLIAMENTARY Report, on the Tobacco Trade. Folio. 3,00. London. 1844. 1844

PARLIAMENTARY Report, on the Coast of Africa. 2 parts. Folio. 1300 pp. 5,00. London.

PARLIAMENTARY Reports. Sixth Annual Report of the Registra General, of British Deaths and Marriages in England. Folio. 1,50. London. 1844

PARLIAMENTARY Reports. First Report of the Commissioners on Improving the Metropolis. Folio. Numerous plates. 3,00. London. 1844

PARLIAMENTARY Report, with Instructions for the Guidance of her Majesty's Naval Officers employed in the suppression of the Slave Trade. Folio. 2,50. London. 1844

PARLIAMENTARY Report of the Children's Employment Commissioners — Mines. Parts I. and II., and Appendix. 3 vols. Folio. 5,50. London. 1842

PARLIAMENTARY Reports. Commercial Tariffs of the World. 14 parts. Folio. 7,50. London. 1841–4

PARLIAMENTARY Reports. Union Workhouses, with Plans. 2 parts. Folio. 1,50. London. 1844

PARLIAMENTARY Reports. Merchant's Seamen's Friend. Folio. ,75. London. 1844

PARLIAMENTARY Reports. Quarantine Regulations. Folio. 2,50. 1836–43

PARLIAMENTARY Report on Building Regulations, &c. Folio. Plates, Plans, &c. 1,25.

PARLIAMENTARY Report on East India Produce. Folio. 2,50. London.

PARLIAMENTARY Report of the Officers of the Railway Departments, with Plates. 2 parts. Folio. 3,00.

PARLIAMENTARY Report respecting Railway Communication between London, Edinburgh and Glasgow. 4 parts, and an Appendix. 9,00.

PARLIAMENTARY Report on the Midland Mines, South Staffordshire. Plates. Folio. 1,50. London. 1843

PARLIAMENTARY Report on Harbors of Refuge, with Plans and Maps. Folio. 1,50. 1845

PARLIAMENTARY Reports. Public Works in Canada. Folio. Maps and Plates. 1,00.

Parliamentary Reports. Age Abstract, Scotland. 2 parts. Folio. 3,00. London. 1843

Parliamentary Report on the Falkland Islands. Folio. ,75. London. 1843

Parliamentary Reports. Statistical Tables by the Lunacy Commissioners. Folio. 1,00. 1844

Parliamentary Report on Joint Stock Companies. 1,00. 1844

Parliamentary Reports. Special Reports of the Indian Law Commissioners. Folio. 2,50. London. 1844

Parliamentary Report on the Fine Arts. 3 parts. 1,00. 1844

Parliamentary Report on the School of Design. 3 parts. ,75. 1845

Parliamentary Report on the Expedition to the River Niger. Folio. 1,00. 1843

Parliamentary Reports. Fifth General Report on Railways. Folio. 2,25. 1844

Parliamentary Report on Shipwrecks. Folio. 3,00. 1844

Parliamentary Report on Smoke Prevention. Folio. 1,50. 1843

Parliamentary Reports. Union Work-Houses in Ireland. 2 parts. 1,50. 1844

Parliamentary Reports. On the Croydon and Epsom Railway, &c. ,75. 1844

Parliamentary Report on Kingston Harbor. Folio. ,50.

Parliamentary Reports. Expository Statement on the New Tariff. Folio. 1,00. 1845

Parliamentary Report on the Health of the Navy. Folio. 2 parts. 3,00. 1830–6

Parliamentary Reports. Enumeration Abstract, England, Wales, and Scotland. 2 parts. Folio. 3,50.

Parliamentary Reports. Occupation Abstract. 1,75.

Parliamentary Reports. Revenue, Population and Commerce of the United Kingdom. Folio. 2,00. 1844

PARLIAMENTARY Report on the Emoluments of Officers of Justice in Scotland. 2 parts. Folio. 1,00.

PARLIAMENTARY Report on Education, with Plans of School-Houses. Part II. Folio. 1,50.

PARLIAMENTARY Reports. Sundry Railroads. Folio. 50 cts. each.

PARLIAMENTARY. First, Second and Third Reports of the Public Works of Ireland, with Plates. 2 thick parts. 7,50.

PARLIAMENTARY Report on Steam Carriages. 1,50.

PARLIAMENTARY Report on the Cheltenham and Great Western Union Railway Bill. 3,00.

PARLIAMENTARY Review (The) for 1826–1828. 8vo. 3,50. London. 1828

PAUL (John.) Parish Officer's Complete Guide. 8vo. 1,25. London. 1774

PAYNE (Joseph.) See *Carrington, Moore, Eng. Com. Law Reports.*

PEAKE (Thomas.) Compendium of the Law of Evidence. 8vo. 2,00. London. 1822

PEAKE (Thomas.) Cases at Nisi Prius in King's Bench, from Sittings after East. Term, 30 Geo. III. to the Sittings after Mich. Term, 35 Geo. III. 8vo. 2,00. London. 1795

PEAKE (Thomas.) Additional Cases at Nisi Prius, being a continuation of Cases at Nisi Prius before Lord Kenyon, and other eminent Judges, taken at different times between the Years 1795 and 1812, by Thomas Peake, Serjeant-at-Law; with Notes, by Thomas Peake, Jr., Esq., of Lincoln's Inn, Barrister at Law. Royal 8vo. Vol. II. 1,00. *bds.* London. 1829

PECK (James H.) Trial of. See *Stansbury.*

PEERE-WILLIAMS (W.) Reports of Cases argued and determined in the High Court of Chancery, and of some Special Cases adjudged in the King's Bench, from 1695 to 1734, with Notes and References by his Son, W. Peere-Williams. Sixth edition, with References to the Proceedings in the Court, and to later Cases, by S. C. Cox; with

Notes and References to the Modern Cases, by J. B. Monro, W. L. Lowndes, and J. Randall. 3 vols. Royal 8vo. 12,50. London. 1826

PEREZIUS (Ant.) Codicis Justiniani. Folio. 3,75. Amsterdam. 1598

PERKINS (John.) Treatise of the Laws of England on Conveyancing. 15th ed. 12mo. 1,50. London. 1827

"A little Treatise of certain titles of the Common Law, wittily and learnedly composed and published in the Reign of King Edward VII."

PERLEY (Jeremiah.) The Maine Justice. 8vo. 1,00. Hallowell. 1829

PETERS (Richard.) Admiralty Decisions in the District Court of Pennsylvania, with an Appendix, containing the Laws of Oleron, of Wisbuy, of the Hanse Towns, &c. &c. 2 vols. 8vo. 5,00. Philadelphia. 1807

PETERS (Richard.) A full and arranged Digest of Cases decided in the Supreme, Circuit and District Courts of the United States, from the Organization of the Government to 1840. 3 vols. 8vo. 12,00. Philadelphia. 1838–40

PETERS (Richard.) Reports of Cases in the Circuit Court of the United States, for the Third Circuit, from 1803 to 1818. 8vo. 4,50. Philadelphia. 1819

PETERS (Richard.) Reports of Cases in the Supreme Court of the United States, from 1828 to 1842. 17 vols. 8vo. Per vol. 4,00. Philadelphia and Boston. 1828–42

PETERS (Richard.) Condensed Reports of Cases in the Supreme Court of the United States, from its Organization to 1827. 6 vols. 8vo. 21,00. Philadelphia. 1830–35

PETERSDORFF (C.) Practical and Elementary Abridgment of the Common Law, as altered and established by the Recent Statutes, Rules of Court, and Modern Decisions; comprising a full Abstract of all Cases argued and determined in the Courts of Common Law and on Appeal, with Rules of Court, from Michaelmas Term, 1824, to Michaelmas Term, 1840, inclusive, and of the Statutes passed during the same Period, with Connecting and Illustrative

References to the Earlier Authorities, and Explanatory Notes; designed either as a Supplement to the Author's Abridgment, or as a separate Work. 5 vols. Royal 8vo. Published at £7 17*s.* 6*d.* *bds.* 20,00. London. 1841–4

PETERSDORFF (C.) Practical and Elementary Abridgment of the Cases argued and determined in the Courts of King's Bench, Common Pleas, Exchequer, and at Nisi Prius, and of the Rules of Court from the Restoration in 1660, &c. 17 vols. Royal 8vo. 75,00. 1829–35

PETIT (M.) Traité des Surenchères. 8vo. *half cf.* 2,25. Paris. 1843

PHILLIPS (S. M.) Treatise on the Law of Evidence; 2d Am. from 3d Lond. ed., with Additional Notes. 2 vols. 8vo. 6,00. New York. 1840

PHILLIPS (Willard.) Treatise on the Law of Insurance. 2d ed. 2 vols. 8vo. 10,00. Boston. 1840

PHILLIPS (Willard.) On the Law of Patents. 3,50. Boston. 1837

PHILLIPS (Willard.) Inventor's Guide, containing the Rules, Forms and Proceedings for securing Patent Rights. 12mo. 1,00. Boston. 1837

PICKERING (Octavius.) Reports of Cases in the Supreme Judicial Court of Massachusetts, from 1822 to 1842. 24 vols. 8vo. Per vol. 4,00. Boston. 1824–42

These Reports form a continuation of the Massachusetts Reports. The variety of cases considered, and the able judgments of the court, give them a high practical value for the profession. Several of the volumes have passed to a second edition, and are enriched by learned annotations by J. G. Perkins, Esq., of the Essex Bar.

Mr. Pickering resigned the office of Reporter in 1839, and was succeeded by T. Metcalf, Esq., who commenced his labors with the March Term, 1840.

PICKERING (Danby.) Statutes at Large, from Magna Charta to the end of the 11th Parliament of Great Britain, 1761. 29 vols. 8vo. (Vol. 24 wanting.) 30,00. London. 1762

PIKE (Albert.) Reports of Cases in the Supreme Court of Arkansas, in Law and Equity. 2 vols. 8vo. 5,00 per vol. Little Rock. 1840–1

PITMAN (E. D.) Treatise on the Law of Principal and Surety. 8vo. 1,50. London. 1840

PLOWDEN (E.) Commentaries or Reports in the Reigns of Edward VI., Mary, Philip and Mary, and Elizabeth, translated with Notes. 2 vols. Royal 8vo. 9,00. London. 1816

PLOWDEN (Francis.) Treatise upon the Law of Usury and Annuities. 8vo. 1,25. London. 1797

PORTALIS (J. E. M.) Discours, Rapports et Traveax Inédites sur le Code Civil. 8vo. 2,25. Paris. 1844

PORTER (Benjamin F.) Reports of Cases at Law and in Equity in the Supreme Court of Alabama. 8vo. Vol. II. 3,00. Tuscaloosa. 1836

PORTER (Benjamin F.) Reports of Cases argued and adjudged in the Supreme Court of Alabama, commencing in 1834. 8vo. 8 vols. 5,00 per vol. Tuscaloosa. 1835–41

POTHIER (M.) Œuvres Complétes. 8vo. *half cf.* 18 vols. 30,00. Paris. 1825

POTHIER (M.) Traités sur différentes Matières de Droit Civil appliquées à l'Usage du Barreau et de Jurisprudence Française, seconde édition, revue. 8 vols. 4to. *half cf.* 25,00. Paris. 1781

POTHIER (R. J.) Treatise on the Law of Obligations or Contracts, translated from the French, with an Introduction, Appendix and Notes, Illustrative of the English Law on the Subject; by William David Evans. 2 vols. 8vo. 8,00. Philadelphia. 1840

POTHIER (R. J.) Treatise on the Contract of Sale. Translated from the French. By L. S. Cushing. 8vo. 2,50. Boston. 1839

"The translator hopes that his work will be found to be exact; he very early, in his professional life, began the study of these writings; he has devoted to it some portion of the leisure hours of many years; and he has aimed, in the following pages, to furnish his professional brethren with a translation, which shall not be unworthy of their approbation or of the fame of the author." — *Preface.*

POTHIER (R. J.) Pandectes de Justinien mises dans un Nouvelle Ordre. 8vo. 24 vols. *half cf.* 48,00. Paris. 1818

Poujol (M.) Traité des Successions, ou Commentaire du Titre 1er du Livre iii. du Code Civil. 2 vols. 8vo. 3,50. Paris. 1837

Powell (John Joseph.) Essay upon the Law of Contracts and Agreements. 2 vols. in 1. 8vo. 3,00. Exeter. 1823

Powell (John Joseph.) Original Precedents in Conveyancing, selected from the Manuscript Collection of J. J. Powell. By Charles Barton. 3 vols. 8vo. 6,75. 2d ed. London. 1810

Powell (John Joseph.) Treatise on Mortgages. 2 vols. 8vo. 2,00. London. 1791

Powell (John Joseph.) Essay on Devises. 8vo. 1,25. New York. 1806

Powell (John Joseph.) Essay on the Learning respecting the Creation and Execution of Powers, &c. 8vo. 1,25. London. 1787

Poynter (Thomas.) The Doctrine and Practice of the Ecclesiastical Courts in Doctor's Commons relative to the Subject of Marriage and Divorce. 2d ed. 8vo. 2,25. London. 1824

Precedents in Chancery, being a Collection of Cases argued and determined in the High Court of Chancery, from the Year 1689 to 1722. 2d ed. 8vo. 3,00. London. 1786

Presentation des Comptes de Finances, Reglement Definitif du Budget de 1827, &c. 4to. 1,25. Paris. 1829

Preston (Richard.) Elementary Treatise on Estates. 2 vols. 8vo. 6,00. London. 1820

Preston (Richard.) An Essay on Abstracts of Title of Laws of Property, stating in detail the Duty of Solicitors in preparing, &c., and of Council in advising, an Abstract of Title. 2 vols. in 1. 8vo. 4,00. New York. 1828

Preston (Richard.) On the Law of Legacies. 8vo. 1,50. London. 1827

Preston (Richard.) A Treatise on Conveyancing. 3 vols. 8vo. 8,00. London. 1819

PRICE (George.) Reports of Cases in the Exchequer and in the Exchequer Chamber, from East. Term, 54 Geo. III., 1841, to the Sittings after Mich. Term, 4 Geo. IV. 1823. 13 vols. in 6. 8vo. Per vol. 3,00. Philadelphia. 1835

PRIESTLEY (Joseph.) Remarks on Blackstone's Commentaries, with Blackstone's Reply, &c. 8vo. 1,50. Philadelphia. 1773

PRINCE (Oliver H.) Digest of the Laws of Georgia, with copious Index ; compiled by order of the Legislature. 2d ed. 8vo. 5,00. Athens, Ga. 1837

PRINCIPLES of Equity (Kames.) 4to. 2,00. Edinburgh. 1760

PRIVILEGIA Londoni, or the Rights, Liberties, Privileges, Laws and Customs of the City of London, containing the Charters granted to the City, &c. 3d ed. 4,00. London. 1723

PROBATE Directory, being the Laws of New Hampshire respecting the Estates of Testators, Intestates and Wards. ,75. Concord, N. H. 1829

PROUDHON (M.) Traité du Domain de Propriété, ou de la Distinction des Biens par rapport au Domain Privé. 8vo. 3,75. Brusselles. 1843

PUBLIC Acts of Congress respecting the Sale and Disposition of the Public Lands. 2 vols. 8vo. 10,50. Washington. 1838

PUFFENDORF (Samuel, Baron,) De Officio Hominis et Civis juxta Legem Naturalem. 2 vols. 8vo. 5,00. Leipsic. 1769

PUFFENDORF (Samuel, Baron.) Another copy. 1,62. Basil. 1739

PUFFENDORF (Samuel, Baron.) Of the Law of Nature and Nations, done from the Latin into English, by Basil Kennet, with the Notes of M. Barbeyrac. 5th ed. Folio. 15,00. London. 1749

PUFFENDORF (Samuel, Baron.) Law of Nature and Nations, abridged from the Original, by J. Spavan. 2 vols. in 1. 1,25. London. 1716

PUFFENDORF De Jure Naturæ et Gentium Libri Octo, cum Commentario Hertii et Aliorum. 2 vols. 4to. 5,50. Frankfort.

RAM (James.) The Science of Legal Judgment. 8vo. 1,00. Philadelphia. 1835

RANKIN (R. R.) An Analysis of the Law of Patents. 12mo. ,50. London. 1824

RASTELL (William.) Collection in English of the Statutes now (1583) in force, continued from the beginning of Magna Charta. 4to. 2,00. London. 1583

RASTELL (William.) Collection of Entries. Folio. 6,00. London. 1651

RASTELL (William.) Same work. 6,50. London. 1574

RAY (Dr. J.) Medical Jurisprudence of Insanity. 12mo. 2,00. Boston. 1844

RAYMOND (James.) Digested Chancery Cases contained in the Reports of the Court of Appeals of Maryland. 8vo. 4,00. Baltimore. 1839

RAYMOND (Robert, Lord.) Reports of Cases in King's Bench and Common Pleas, temp. Will. III., Anne, Geo. I. and Geo. II.; by Geo. Wilson. 2d ed. 2 vols. Folio. 4,50. London. 1743

RAYMOND (Sir Thomas.) Reports of Cases in the King's Bench, Common Pleas, temp. Car. II. 8vo. 2,75. London. 1793

REBUFFIUS (Peter.) Commentaries, &c. Folio. 2,50. Amsterdam. 1668

REDESDALE (Lord.) See *Mitford.*

REEVES (John.) History of the Law of Shipping and Navigation. 8vo. 2,50. London. 1792

REEVES (J.) Two Tracts, showing that Americans born before the Independence are, by the Law of England, not Aliens. 8vo. ,50. 1816

REFLEXIONS sur l'État Actuel du Jury, de la Liberté Individuelle et des Prisons. 8vo. 1,50. Paris. 1818

REGISTRUM Brevium tam Originalium quam Judicialium. 4th ed. Folio. 4,00. London. 1687

REINHARD (Charles de) and M'LELLAN (A.) Report of the Trials of, at Quebec, for Murder. 8vo. 1,25. Montreal. 1818

RENOUARD (A. C.) Traité des Droits d'Auteurs dans la Littérature, les Sciences et les Beaux-Arts. 2 vols. 8vo. 4,50. Paris. 1839

REPERTORIUM Juridicum. General Index to all the Cases in the Year Books, Entries, Reports and Abridgments in Law and Equity, beginning with Edward I., and continued down to this Time; containing nearly 40,000 Cases, &c. &c. Folio. 3,75. London. 1742

REPORT of a Select Committee to the House of Commons, on Lights, Harbor Dues and Pilotage. Folio. 3,50. London. 1822

REPORT of a Select Committee on Duties, Salaries, and Emoluments of Officers, Clerks, and Ministers of Justice of Courts in Scotland. 1,50.

REPORT of a Select Committee on Duties, Salaries, Officers, of the several Courts of Justice in England. Folio. 1,75. London. 1818

REPORT of a Select Committee on the Discretionary Power vested in the Servants of the Crown. Folio. ,50. London. 1832

REPORT of a Select Committee on Emigration. ,50. 1832

REPORT (First) of the Prison Discipline Society. 6th ed. 8vo. 3,00. Boston. 1830

REPORTS of Cases in Law and Equity, argued and determined in the Supreme Court of Alabama. New Series. 3 vols. 15,00. Tuscaloosa. 1841–2

REPORTS of Her Majesty's Poor Law Commissioners. 11 vols. 8vo. 5,50. London. 1842

REPORTS of the Select Committee on Finance. 4 vols. 8vo. 4,00. London. 1798

REPORTS of Cases in Chancery in the Reign of Charles I.,

and to the 20th of Charles II. 3 vols. 8vo. 5,00. London. 1693

Revised Statutes of Massachusetts, passed Nov. 4, 1835. By Theron Metcalf and Horace Mann. 8vo. 3,00. Boston. 1836

Revised Statutes of Massachusetts. An Annual Supplement is published, edited by T. Metcalf, Esq.

Revised Statutes of the State of New York, including the Statutory Provisions of a general nature, passed from 1828 to 1835, inclusive, and all the Acts of general interest passed 1836. 3 vols. 8vo. 13,50. Albany. 1836

Revised Statutes of the State of Vermont, passed Nov. 19, 1839. Published by the Legislature. 8vo. 3,50. Burlington. 1840

Rhode Island. Public Laws; with the Charter, &c. 8vo. 2,00. Providence. 1839

Ricard (Samuel.) Traité Général du Commerce. 2 vols. 4to. 2,00. Amsterdam. 1781

Richardson (Robert.) On Wills. 8vo. 2,00. London. 1769

Richardson (Robert.) Attorney's Practice in the Court of Common Pleas. 5th ed. 2 vols. 8vo. 9,00. London.

Richer (F.) Traité de la Mort Civile. 4to. *cf.* 2,25. Paris. 1755

Ridgeway (William.) Reports of Cases upon Appeals, and Writs of Error in the High Court of Parliament in Ireland, since the Restoration of the Appellate Jurisdiction. 3 vols. 8vo. 8,00. Dublin. 1795

Ridgeway (William.) See *Irish Term Reports.*

Ritson (J.) Maxims in Conveyancing. 1 vol. ,75. London. 1804

Robernier (F. de.) De la Preuve du Droit de Propriété en fait d'Immeubles, etc. 2 vols. 8vo. 4,50. Paris. 1843

Roberts (William.) Treatise on the Statute of Frauds, with a Dissertation upon the Admission of Parol Evidence to explain Written Instruments. 3d Am. from the last London edition, with References to, and a Digest of the American Decisions, and the late Decisions in Great Britain ; and an Appendix, showing the extent of the Adoption of the Statute of 29 Car. II. c. 3, in the several States of the Union. 8vo. 3,00. Philadelphia. 1833

ROBERTS (William.) Treatise on the Construction of the Statutes 13 Eliz. c. 5, and 27 Eliz. c. 4, relating to Voluntary and Fraudulent Conveyances. 8vo. 2,25. Burlington, Vt. 1845

ROBINSON (Christopher.) Reports of Cases in the Admiralty, from Mich. Term, 1798 to 1808. 6 vols. 8vo. 18,00. New York. 1800–10

ROBINSON (William.) The Introduction of a Justice of the Peace to the Court of Quarter Sessions. 2 vols. 8vo. 5,00. London. 1836

ROBINSON (William, LL. D.) Formularies, or the Magistrate's Assistant, being a Collection of Precedents for a Justice of the Peace. 2 vols. 8vo. 4,50. London. 1827

ROCCUS (Franciscus.) A Manual of Maritime Law, &c. translated with Notes, by Joseph Reed Ingersol. 8vo. 1,00. Philadelphia. 1809

ROGERS (Daniel.) New York City Hall Recorder. 1816–17. 6 vols. in 3. 10,00. New York. 1817

ROGERS (Abner, Jr.) Report of the Trial of Abner Rogers, Jr., indicted for the Murder of Charles Lincoln, Jr., late Warden of the Massachusetts State Prison ; before the Supreme Judicial Court of Massachusetts, holden at Boston, January 30th, 1844. By George Tyler Bigelow and George Bemis, Esquires, Counsel for the Defendant. 8vo. 1,50. Boston. 1844

"As a case involving the issue of feigned or real insanity, we believe the present the most interesting on record, certainly in English or American jurisprudence."

ROGRON (J. A.) Codes Français expliqués par leur Motifs, &c. 2 parts. 4to. 9,50. Paris. 1843

ROGRON (J. A.) Code de Commerce expliqué par ses Motifs, par des Examples et par la Jurisprudence. 12mo. 2,00. Paris. 1841

ROGRON (J. A.) Codes d'Instruction Criminelle et Penal expliqués. 2 vols. 12mo. 5,00. Paris. 1839

ROGRON (J. A.) Code Civil expliqué. 12mo. 2,50. Paris. 1840

ROOT (Jesse.) Reports of Cases in the Superior Court and in the Superior Court of Errors of Connecticut, from 1789 to 1798. 2 vols. 8vo. 5,00. Hartford. 1798–1802

ROPER (R. S. Donnison.) Treatise upon the Law of Legacies. 3d ed., with a new Arrangement and Additions, by Henry Hopely White. 2 vols. 8vo. 8,00. Philadelphia. 1829

ROSCOE (Henry.) Digest of the Law of Evidence at the Trial of Actions at Nisi Prius. 1st Am. from 2d London ed., with Notes by James Bayard. 8vo. 3,50. Philadelphia. 1836

ROSCOE (Henry.) Digest of the Law of Evidence in Criminal Cases, with Notes and References to American Decisions, and to the English Common Law and Ecclesiastical Reports, by George Sharswood. 8vo. 5,50. Philadelphia. 1840

ROSS (George.) Treatise on the Law of Vendors and Purchasers of Personal Property. 8vo. 2,50. London. 1841

ROSSI (M. P.) Traité de Droit Pénal. 8vo. 2,25. Bruxelles. 1841

ROUSE (C. W. B.) Dissertation concerning the Landed Property of Bengal. 8vo. 1,50. London. 1791

RUGGLES (Thomas.) The Barrister, or Strictures on Education.

RUNNINGTON (Charles.) History, Principles, and Practice of the Legal Remedy by Ejectment, and the resulting Action for Mesne Profits. 1st Am. ed. 8vo. 2,50. New York. 1806

RUSSELL (William Oldnall.) Treatise on Crimes and Misdemeanors, by Charles Sprengel Greaves. Fifth American from the third London ed. Very greatly enlarged.

With the Notes and References of Daniel Davis and Theron Metcalf, Esqs., and additional Notes and References, by George Sharswood. 2 vols. super-royal 8vo. 10,00. Now for the *first* time reprinted in *full*. Philadelphia. 1845

RUSSELL (William Oldnall,) and RYAN (E.) Crown Cases reserved for consideration, and decided by the twelve Judges of England, from the year 1799 to 1824. 8vo. 4,00. London. 1825

RUSSELL (James.) Reports in the High Court of Chancery during the time of Lord Chancellor Eldon, and 7th Geo. IV. 4 vols. 8vo. 20,00. New York and London. 1828

RUSSELL (W.) Treatise on the Reform Act, 2 Will. IV. c. 45, with Practical Directions to Overseers and Town-Clerks, and a Copy of the Order in Council of the 11th July, 1832; also, an Appendix containing a Copy of the Act, and also the Boundary Act, 2 & 3 Will. IV. c. 64. 12mo. ,75. London. 1832

RUTHERFORTH (T.) Institutes of Natural Law, being the Substance of a Course of Lectures on Grotius de Jure Belli et Pacis. 2d Am. ed. 8vo. 3,50. Baltimore. 1832

RYLAND (Archer.) The Crown Circuit Companion, in which is incorporated the Crown Circuit Assistant. 10th ed. 8vo. 2,00. London. 1836

RYLEY (William.) Placita Parliamentaria. Folio. 2,50. London. 1661

SALKELD (William.) Reports of Cases in the King's Bench, from 1 Wm. et Mar. to 10 Ann. Best ed. 2 vols. in 1. Folio. 5,50. London. 1773

SALKELD (William.) Another copy. 4th ed. by D'Anvers. 2 vols. Folio. 7,50. 1742

SALKELD (William.) Another copy. 4th ed., by D'Anvers. 3 vols. Folio. 9,00. 1742

SALKELD (William.) Another copy. 3 vols. 8vo. Philadelphia. 12,00. 1822

SAMPSON (William.) Discourse, &c., on the History of the Law 8vo. 1,00. Washington, D. C. 1826

SANDERS (Francis Williams.) Essay on Uses and Trusts, and on the Nature and Operation of Conveyances at Common Law, and those deriving their effect from the Statute of Uses. 1st Am. from 4th London ed. 8vo. 3,50. Philadelphia. 1830

SANDERS (Francis Williams.) Same. 5th ed., by G. W. Sanders and J. Warner. 2 vols. 8vo. *bds.* 9,00. London. 1844

SAUNDERS (Sir Edmund.) Reports in King's Bench temp. Car. II. 2 vols. Folio. 3,50. London. 1722

SAUNDERS (Sir Edmund.) The same. 1st Am. from the 3d London ed. 3 vols. 8vo. 7,50. Philadelphia. 1807

SAUNDERS (Sir Edmund.) The same. 4th Am. from last London ed. By John Patterson and Ed. Vaughan Williams. 3 vols. 8vo. 12,00. New York. 1833

SAUNDERS (John Simcoe.) Law of Pleading and Evidence in Civil Actions, arranged alphabetically; with practical Forms. 2 vols. 8vo. 7,50. Philadelphia. 1837

SAVIGNY (Frederick Charles.) The Vocation of our Age for Legislation and Jurisprudence. Translated by Abraham Heyward. 8vo. 2,25. (Privately printed.) London.

SAVIGNY (C. Von.) The History of the Roman Law during the Middle Ages, translated from the German by E. Cathcart. 8vo. 3,50. London. 1829

SAYER (Joseph.) Law of Costs, &c. 8vo. 1,00. London. 1768

SAYER (Joseph.) Law of Damages. 12mo. 1,25. Dublin. 1792

SAYER (Joseph.) Reports of Cases adjudged in the Court of King's Bench, 25 Geo. II. 30 Geo. II. Folio. 2,25. London. 1775

SCAMMON (J. Y.) Reports of cases argued and determined in the Supreme Court of the State of Illinois. 4 vols. 20,00. Philadelphia and Boston. 1841–4

SCHOALES (John,) and LEFROY (Thomas.) Reports of Cases in Chancery in Ireland, temp. Lord Redesdale, from 1802 to 1806. 2 vols. 8vo. 7,50. New York. 1808–11

Schôell (F.) Histoire abregé des Traités de Paix entre les Puissances de l'Europe depuis la Paix de Westphalie. 8vo. 3,00. Brussells. 1837

Schomberg (Alexander C.) Historical and Chronological View of Roman Law. 8vo. 1,50. Oxford. 1785

Scrivener's Guide. 2 vols. 8vo. 4,00. London. 1740

Sea Laws. A general Treatise on the Dominion of the Sea; and a complete Body of the Sea Laws. 4to. 2,50. London. 1703

Seaton (Henry Wilmot.) Forms of Decrees in Equity. 8vo. 2,25. New York. 1831

Secret Debates and Proceedings of the Convention assembled at Philadelphia in 1787, for the purpose of forming the Constitution of the United States. 8vo. 1,25. Washington. 1836

Selden (John.) Mare Clausum, or the Right and Dominion of the Sea. In two Books. Folio. 4,50. London. 1663

Selden (John.) The same. *old calf.* 2,83. London. 1663

Selden (John.) Law Tracts. Folio. 2,83. London. 1683

Selden (John.) Opera Omnia, tam edita quam inedita, collegit, ae recensuit Vitam Auctoris, etc. David Wilkins, S. T. P. 6 vols. Folio. *calf.* 36,00. London. 1726

Selden (John.) De Jure Naturæ et Gentium. Folio. 3,00. London. 1640

Selden (John.) English Janus. Folio. 2,50. London. 1682

Select Cases adjudged in the Courts of New York, containing the Case of J. V. N. Yates, and the Case of the Journeymen Cordwainers of New York. 8vo. 2,00. New York. 1811

Selections from the Laws of England. 2 vols. 8vo. 3,00. London. 1806

Selfridge (Thomas O.) Trial of, for killing C. Austin. 8vo. 1,50. Boston. 1806

Sellon (John Baker.) Practice of the Courts of King's Bench and Common Pleas, originally compiled by Crompton. 2 vols. 8vo. 7,50. New York. 1813

SELWYN (William.) Abridgment of the Law of Nisi Prius With Notes by Henry Wheaton. 4th Am. from 7th London ed. 2 vols. 8vo. 10,00. Philadelphia. 1839

SERGEANT (Thomas.) Treatise upon the Law of Pennsylvania relative to the Proceedings by Foreign Attachment, with the Acts of Assembly now in force on the Subject. 8vo. 3,50. Philadelphia. 1840

SERGEANT (Thomas.) Land Law of Pennsylvania. 8vo. 2,50. Philadelphia. 1838

SERGEANT (Thomas.) Constitutional Law, being a View of the Practice and Jurisdiction of the Courts of the United States, and of Constitutional Points decided. 2d ed. with additions. 8vo. 3,00. Philadelphia. 1830

SERGEANT (Thomas.) Select Speeches of. 8vo. 1,50. Philadelphia. 1832

SERGEANT (Thomas.) See *Eng. Com. Law Reports.*

SERGEANT (Henry J.) Treatise on the Lein of Mechanics and Material Men in Pennsylvania, with the Acts of Assembly relating thereto, and various Forms of Claims. 12mo. 1,00. Philadelphia. 1839

SHELFORD (Leonard.) Practical Treatise on the Law of Wills. 12mo. 1,25. London. 1838

SHEPLEY (John.) Reports of Cases argued and determined in the Supreme Judicial Court of the State of Maine, Vols. I.—IX. 3,75 per vol. Hallowell. 1837–44

SHEPPARD. Touchstone of Common Assurances, or a plain and familiar Treatise, opening the Learning of the Common Assurances or Conveyances of the Kingdom. From the last London edition, by Edward Hilliard, and a copious index by Richard Preston. 2 vols. 8vo. 5,00 Philadelphia. 1840

SHEPPARD. Touchstone — the same by Atherly. 2 vols. 5,00. London. 1820

SHEPPARD. Touchstone — the same, by Preston 2 vols. 8vo. *calf.* 10,00. London. 1820

SHERIDAN (John.) The Practice of the King's Bench. 8vo. 4,50. Dublin. 1792

SHERMAN (Henry.) Analytical Digest of the Law of Marine Insurance. 8vo. 3,50. New York. 1841

SHOWER (Sir Bartholomew.) Cases in Parliament, resolved upon Petitions and Writs of Error. Folio. 2,00. London. 1698

SHOWER (Sir Bartholomew.) Another copy. Folio. 1,75. *bds.* 1740

SHOWER (Sir Bartholomew.) The same, with Notes by Leach. 2 vols. 8vo. 8,00. London. 1794

SHOWER (Sir Bartholomew.) Reports of Cases in the King's Bench, temp. Car. II., Jac. II., and Will. III. 2d ed. By Thomas Leach. 2 vols. Folio. 10,50. London. 1708-20

SIDERFIN (Thomas.) Les Reports des divers Special Cases en le Court del Bank Le Roy, &c. les premiers 10 ans. de Charles II. Folio. 2 vols. 6,00. London. 1683

SIMMONS (T. F.) Remarks on the Constitution and Practice of Courts Martial, with a Summary of the Law of Evidence, as connected with such Courts; also, some Notice of the Criminal Law of England, with reference to the 102d Article of War. 3d ed. 8vo. 5,50. London. 1843

SKELTON (W. B.) The Circuit Manual, relative to Indictable Offences. 12mo. 1,62. Dublin. 1844

SMEDES (W. C.) and MARSHALL (T. A.) Reports of Cases in the High Court of Errors and Appeals for the State of Mississippi. 8vo. Vols. I. II. III. IV. 5,00 per vol. Boston. 1843-45

SMITH (J. S.) Treatise on the Practice of the Court of Chancery, with an Appendix, &c. 2 vols. 8vo. 6,00. Philadelphia. 1842

SMITH (John William.) Compendium of Mercantile Law. 8vo. 2,75. Philadelphia. 1841

SMITH (John William.) A Selection of leading Cases on various Branches of the Law, with Notes. 2d ed. 2 vols. royal 8vo. 6,00. Philadelphia. 1844

SMITH (John P.) Reports of Cases in King's Bench and in Chancery, 1803-4. 2d ed. 2 vols. 6,00. London. 1806

SMYTH (Hamilton.) The Office of Justice of the Peace in Ireland. 8vo. 5,50. Dublin. 1841.

SMYTH (Hamilton.) The Law of Landlord and Tenant in Ireland. 8vo. 750. Dublin. 1842

SOLICITOR'S Complete Guide in the Practice of the High Court of Chancery. 2 vols. 12mo. 1,00. London. 1776

SOMMERS (Lord.) On the Rights, Power, and Prerogative of Kings, and the Privileges of the People. 12th ed. 8vo. 1,00. Newport, R. I. 1774

SOUTHARD (Samuel L.) Reports of Cases in the Supreme Court of New Jersey, from 1816 to 1818. 8vo. 3,00. Trenton. 1819

SOUTH CAROLINA. Reports of Judicial Decisions in the Constitutional Court of South Carolina in 1812–16, and, of the Court of Equity for 1822. 2 vols. 8vo. 7,00. Charleston. 1823

SOUTH CAROLINA. Statutes at Large of South Carolina. Edited under the authority of the Legislature by Thomas Cooper. 2 vols. 8vo. Columbia. 1837

SPARKS (Jared.) Diplomatic Correspondence of the American Revolution. 12 vols. 8vo. *calf.* 18,00. Boston. 1829

SPEARS (R. H.) Reports of Cases at Law, in the Court of Appeals of South Carolina, from 1842–44. 2 vols. 8vo. 12,00. Columbia. 1844

SQUAREY (C. W.) A Collection of all the General Rules for Regulating the Practice of the Superior Court; with a copious Index. 12mo. *bds.* ,75. London. 1833

STANSBURY (Arthur J.) Report of the Trial of Judge James H. Peck, on an Impeachment by the House of Representatives of the United States. 8vo. 5,00. Boston. 1833

"This volume contains a great amount of learning in regard to contempts of court, libels, and impeachments, subjects upon which the counsel on both sides exhibit proofs of very diligent research. It will be a valuable repository of authority and argument, in future cases, in which the right of courts to punish contempts may be brought in question."

STARKIE (Thomas.) Reports of Cases at Nisi Prius in

King's Bench and Common Pleas, from Sittings after Mich. Term, 55 Geo. III. 1814, to the Sittings after Mich. Term, 60 Geo. III. 1819. 2 vols. 8vo. 6,00. Exeter, N. H. 1823

STARKIE (Thomas.) Practical Treatise of the Law of Evidence, and Digest of Proofs in Civil and Criminal Proceedings. 7th Am. from the 3d London edition. With the Notes and References to American Decisions, by Theron Metcalf and Benjamin Gerhard. 3 vols. 8vo. 14,00. Philadelphia. 1842

STARKIE (Thomas.) The same. 3 vols. 8vo. 12,00. Published at £4 14*s*. 6*d*. London. 1842

STARKIE (Thomas.) A Treatise on the Law of Slander, with Notes, &c. by John L. Wendell. 2 vols. 8vo. 6,00. Albany. 1843

STARKIE (Thomas.) Treatise on Criminal Pleading, with Precedents of Indictments, Special Pleas, &c. 2d ed. with Additions and Notices of the late Acts for the Amendment of the Criminal Law. 2 vols. 8vo. 4,00. *bds.* London. 1828

STARKIE (Thomas.) The same. 2 vols. 8vo. 4,00. London. 1837

STATE PAPERS and Public Documents of the United States, from the Accession of George Washington to the Presidency, exhibiting a complete View of our Foreign Relations since that Time. 3d ed. Including Confidential Documents, &c. Wait's ed. 12 vols. 8vo. 18,00. Boston. 1819

STATE PAPERS. American Documents, Legislative and Executive, of the Congress of the United States, from the first session of the first, to the third Session of the thirteenth Congress, inclusive; selected and edited, under the authority of Congress, by W. Lowrie and M. St. Clair Clarke. 21 vols. Folio. 120,00. Washington.

STATE TRIALS, a Collection of, and Proceedings upon, High Treason and other Crimes and Misdemeanors, from the Reign of Richard II. to Geo. III. 11 vols. Folio. 22,00. London. 1742

STATE TRIALS, from 1660 to 1681. Folio. 2,00. London. 1678

STATE TRIALS, from the Reign of Henry IV. to the End of the reign of Queen Anne. 4 vols. Folio. 7,00 London. 1719

STATE TRIALS. See *Hargrave.*

STATUTES of the United States. See *Laws of United States.*

STATUTE Laws of the State of Connecticut, compiled in obedience to a Resolve of the General Assembly, passed May, 1835. 8vo. 2,50. Hartford. 1835

STATUTES relating to the Admiralty, Navy, and Ships of War, &c., down to the 14th Year of King Geo. II. 4to. 2,00. Boston. 1755

STATUTES of Tennessee, of a general and permanent Nature, from the Commencement of the Government to the present Time. 8vo. 6,00. Nashville. 1836

STATUTES of Ohio. 5,00. 8vo. Columbus. 1841

STAUNTON (Sir George T.) The Fundamental Laws, and a Selection from the Supplementary Statutes of the Penal Code of China. Translated from the Chinese. 4to. *Russia gilt.* 8,00. London. 1810

STEARNS (Asahel.) Summary of the Law and Practice of Real Actions, with an Appendix of Practical Forms. 8vo. 4,00. Hallowell. 1831

STEARNS (Asahel.) See *Massachusetts Laws.*

STEPHEN (John Henry.) Treatise on the Principles of Pleading in Civil Actions; comprising a Summary View of the whole Proceedings in a Suit at Law 8vo. 3,00. Philadelphia. 1840

STEPHEN (John Henry.) The same. 1st ed. 3,50. London.

STEPHEN (Henry J.) New Commentaries on the Laws of England, partly founded on Blackstone. 4 vols. 12,00. New York. 1843-6

STEPHENS (Archibald J.) Law of Nisi Prius Evidence in Civil Actions, and Arbitrations and Awards. With Notes, by George Sharswood. 3 vols. 8vo. 15,00. Philadelphia. 1844

STEVENS (Robert) and BENECKE (William.) Treatise on Average and Adjustments of Losses in Marine Insurance; with Notes by Willard Phillips. 8vo. 3,00. Boston. 1833

STEWART (George N.) and PORTER (Benjamin F.) Reports of Cases at Law and in Equity in the Supreme Court of Alabama. 8vo. 5 vols. 25,00. Tuscaloosa. 1836–7

STEWART (James.) Reports of Cases in the Vice-Admiralty of Nova Scotia, from 1803 to 1813, 8vo. 4,50. London. 1814

STOCK (J. S.) Practical Treatise on the Law of Non Compotes Mentis, or Persons of Unsound Mind. 8vo. 1,75. Philadelphia. 1839

STOKES (Anthony.) View of the Constitution of the British Colonies in North America at the Time the War broke out. 8vo. 2,00. London. 1783

STORY (Joseph.) Selection of Pleadings in Civil Actions, with Annotations. 2d ed., with Additions by Benjamin L. Oliver. 8vo. 5,00. Boston. 1829

STORY (Joseph.) Discourse upon the Inauguration of the Author as Dane Professor of Law in Harvard University. 8vo. ,25. Boston. 1829

STORY (Joseph.) Commentaries on the Law of Bailments, with Illustrations from the Civil and the Foreign Law. 4th ed. 8vo. 5,00. Boston. 1846

"All the cases, deemed worthy of any notice, in the English and American law, and all the best authorities in the civil and foreign law, are quoted and commented upon. Those cases and authorities, which are contradictory, are critically examined, and such as are sound, or as have been established as law, are distinguished from those which are erroneous, or have been doubted, or overruled. The principles, which have been adopted and established in each of these various systems of jurisprudence, under each branch of the law of bailments, are presented to the reader at one view, and may serve as a perpetual commentary upon each other. Everything, regarding this subject, which is really valuable, in either system, may be found in this work. The plan and execution of it deserve the highest commendation. It is a book, which, for its intrinsic merit, and preëminent utility, will readily find its way into the library of every accomplished practical lawyer, and for its various learning and sound doctrines, will be read and admired by every learned jurist."

STORY (Joseph.) Commentaries on the Constitution of the United States, with a Preliminary Review of the Constitutional History of the Colonies and States before the Adoption of the Constitution. 3 vols. 8vo. 12,00. Boston. 1833

" A long and elaborate review of this work has appeared in the *Critical Review of Legislation and Jurisprudence*, a periodical published at Heidelburg, Germany, by two celebrated jurists, Messrs. Mittemaier and Zachariæ. In the course of the article the reviewer says, 'we have in the present work as perfect and excellent a commentary upon the North American public law, as can be produced by deep and profound reflection, acute logic, extensive knowledge of the national condition and writings and just political views; and consequently the author has, in a great degree, removed the difficulties in the way of the acquisition of an accurate knowledge of the American public law. Professor Story, by his talented and diligent labors, has, without doubt, done a great service, not only to his countrymen, but also, and in a still higher degree, to the European publicists, among whom his work will receive an honorable fame, as readily awarded as it will be enduring.' "

STORY (Joseph.) The same, abridged by the Author. 8vo. 3,00. Boston. 1833

The *Revue Etrangere*, published at Paris, says that "a good French translation of this Abridgment would be a service rendered to all the continent of Europe."

STORY (Joseph.) Commentaries on the Conflict of Laws, Foreign and Domestic. 2d ed. 8vo. 6,50. Boston. 1841

This work has been reprinted in England, has been translated into German; and we have understood that a translation is now preparing into French. It has been extensively reviewed in Europe. The following are extracts from some of the reviews:

Extract of a letter from J. FERGUSSON, Esq. late Judge in the Consistorial Court of Scotland, and author of the work on Divorce.

"I have repeatedly and deliberately gone through the whole work of Mr. Justice Story, which I deem the most comprehensive and candid in our language, relating to that department of the law administered so long by the Consistory Court of Edinburgh as the Inferior, and the Court of Session as the Grand Consistory of this kingdom. No jurist can peruse it, without admiration of the industry, candor and learning with which it is composed.

"If you can attract the attention certainly merited to this work, it must be useful in dispelling prejudices and exciting imitation. For it supplies valuable information, supported by a greater body of authorities, both in opinions of the most eminent jurists, and in decisions of consistorial judicatures, than I have ever before seen collected in one volume."

"Dr. Story's work is altogether of so excellent a description, and betokens a mind so completely embued with the purest principles of legal philosophy, that it ought to be in the hands of every person who aims at studying, in an intelligent way, the higher departments of professional knowledge." — *Edinburgh Law Journal*, No. XI.

"Professor Story has long been known to the jurists of every country in Europe, as one of the few great masters of the science of jurisprudence that the world at present possesses, and one who has been mainly instrumental in pushing forward those legal reforms, which have of late years done honor to the United States. We hail the work of Professor Story not merely on account of its intrinsic beauties, but also as a means of promoting an interest in the study of jurisprudence. The power with which he has balanced conflicting arguments, and the learning which he has displayed in travelling through the heavy labors of his predecessors, and extracting from them the pith of their reasoning, must delight every inquisitive mind, and justify us in a hope, which they who peruse the book will not think extravagant, that the Treatise on the Conflict of Laws may prove the foundation, in this country, of a school of jurisprudence." — *London Legal Examiner.*

"This is a remarkable work, calculated to excite the most lively interest in both hemispheres. We exceedingly regret that our limits do not allow us to analyze each chapter by itself; we have found, upon all the matters of international law, the discussions perfectly reasoned and supported by authorities." — *From a French Journal, the Revue Etrangere, for Oct.* 1834.

A highly complimentary review of this work is to be found in the *Critical Journal for Jurisprudence and Legislation of Foreign Countries*, edited at Heidelburg, in Germany, by Messrs. Mittemaier and Zachariæ, two of the first jurists in Germany.

In a late case before the English Court of Common Pleas, (*Huber* v. *Steiner*, 2 Bing. N. C. 211) Lord Chief Justice Tindall cites Mr. Justice Story's Commentaries on the Conflict of Laws, and speaks of them as "a work which it would be unjust to notice, without, at the same time, a tribute to the learning, acuteness and accuracy of its author."

STORY (Joseph.) Commentaries on Equity Jurisprudence, as administered in England and America. 2 vols. 8vo. 4th ed. 11,00. Boston. 1846

A work like the present has been very much wanted by the profession in our country. No complete treatise on the subject of Equity Jurisprudence, embracing all the English and American cases, has ever appeared before in the United States. Mr. Justice Story, after having elaborately traced the origin of Equity or Chancery, and determined its meaning — a topic having much intrinsic difficulty, and very imperfectly treated by previous writers — proceeds to consider the various subject-matters over which the jurisdiction of the courts of equity is exercised. He first treats of the important matters arising out of *Accident;* next, of *Mistake*, under which head are considered the difficult questions arising from *ignorance of law.* The next chapter relates to *Actual* or *Positive Fraud;* the next embraces the vast field of *Constructive Fraud;* under which head are considered the questions arising from the judiciary relations of *client* and *attorney*, *guardian* and *ward*, *trustee* and *cestui que trust*, &c., the subject of *Fraudulent Conveyances*, *Registrative*, *Notice*, *Tacking*, &c. The next chapter relates to matters arising from *Account*, as *Appointment*, *General Average*, *Contribution between Sureties*, *Liens*, *Rents and Profits*, *Waste*, *Tithes and Moduses*. The important subject of *Administration*, embracing the whole doctrine of *Marshalling* of *Assets*, is treated in the next chapter. The succeeding chapters of the first volume relate to *Legacies*, *Confusion of Boundaries*, *Dower*, *Marshalling of Securities*, *Partition*, *Partnership*, *Rents*.

STORY (Joseph.) Commentaries on Equity Pleadings and the Incidents thereto, according to the Practice of the Courts of Equity of England and America. 3d ed. 8vo. 6,00. Boston. 1844

"In point of learning and research, it will bear a comparison with any of the elaborate works already published by its author, and that, as a practical manual for consultation and reference, it renders all other works of the kind superfluous and unnecessary, as it contains all that is to be found in them, and much that is new."

"We cordially recommend the work to readers of every denomination. It is so written as to be intelligible and instructive to the mere beginner, while, at the same time, it contains a store of learning, from which even the greatest masters of their profession need not be ashamed to draw. We should have inserted a much longer notice of it, were we not sure that its intrinsic merits will obtain for it a higher place in the estimation of the reader than can possibly be conferred by the eulogium of a critic." — *Am. Jur.*

STORY (Joseph.) Commentaries on the Law of Agency as a Branch of Commercial and Maritime Jurisprudence, with occasional Illustrations from the Civil and Foreign Law. 2d ed. 8vo. 5,00. Boston. 1844

"The whole work is marked with that ample and redundant learning and vigorous good sense, which have given his previous legal writings so high an authority both in England and America. He has everywhere illustrated the doctrines of the common law by copious extracts from distinguished writers on Roman and continental law, and shown us how inevitably the exigences of commerce, and the sense which intelligent merchants have of their own true interests, lead to the same principles in commercial law in England, Scotland, France, and America." — *Am. Jur.*

Story (Joseph.) Commentaries on the Law of Bills of Exchange, Foreign and Inland, as administered in England and America. 8vo. 5,50. Boston. 1843

"The present work embodies much learning derived from foreign sources, usually unexplored by the writers and practisers of Westminster Hall. Among the most important of these are the volumes of Savary, Pothier, Pardessus, and Heineccius. From the latter most distinguished jurist, the author has borrowed a motto, which declares the existence, to a certain extent, of a *common law* on the subject of Bills of Exchange, throughout the civilized world; *Quamvis vero tot Gentium, Civitatumque Leges Cambiales non per omnia conveniant, sunt tamen quædam omnibus communia.* The circumstance, that the principles which govern bills of exchange are common to so many nations, gives a treatise on this subject a value beyond that which attaches to the treatment of merely municipal jurisprudence."

"The present work, though not so large as that of Mr. Chitty, contains all the essential doctrines on the subject, carefully arranged, and established on their proper principles. Nothing is more grateful to the student of the law, than to be able to discern the reason on which rules are founded. Then he may truly hail 'the gladsome light of jurisprudence,' which his great master, Lord Coke, was so fond of contemplating. In the treatise before us, as in all that have preceded it from the same source, the author has constantly aimed to present the principles of the law. But the work has the additional practical value derived from the collection and proper arrangement of the authorities bearing on the subject." — *N. Amer. Review, April,* 1843.

Story (Joseph.) Commentaries on the Law of Promissory Notes and Guaranties of Notes and Checks on Banks and Banking, with occasional Illustrations from the Commercial Law of the Nations of Continental Europe. 8vo. 5,50. Boston. 1845

STORY (Joseph.) Commentaries on the Law of Partnership as a Branch of Commercial and Maritime Jurisprudence, with occasional Illustrations from the Civil and Foreign Law. 8vo. 5,50. Boston. 1841

STORY (Joseph.) See *Abbott*.

STORY (William W.) A Treatise on the Law of Contracts not under Seal. 8vo. 4,50. Boston. 1844

STORY (William W.) Reports of Cases argued and determined in the Circuit Court of the United States for the First Circuit. 2 vols. 8vo. 12,00. Boston. 1842

STRAFFORD (Sir Thomas Wentworth, Earl of.) Trial of, for High Treason. By J. Rushworth. Folio. 2,50. London. 1680

STRANGE (Sir John.) Reports of Cases in Chancery, King's Bench, Common Pleas, and Exchequer, from Trin. Term, 2d Geo. I. to Trin. Term, 21st Geo. II. 2 vols. Folio. 6,00. London. 1755

STUART (George Okill.) Reports of Cases in the Courts of King's Bench, and Courts of Appeals in the Provincial Courts of Lower Canada, from 1810 to 1835. 8vo. 5,00. Quebec. 1834

STUBBS (W.) and TALMASH (G.) Crown Circuit Companion. 8vo. 2,50. Dublin. 1791

STUDY and Practice of the Law, considered in their various Relations to Society. In a Series of Letters. By a Member of Lincoln's Inn. 8vo. 1,25. Portland. 1806

SUGDEN (Edward Burtenshaw.) Practical Treatise of Powers. 8vo. 4th ed. 4,50. London. 1826

SUGDEN (Edward Burtenshaw.) Practical Treatise of the Law of Vendors and Purchasers of Estates. From the 10th London ed. With Notes and References. 3 vols. 6,00. Brookfield, Mass. 1843

SUGDEN (Edward Burtenshaw.) Letters to a Man of Property, on the Sale, Purchase, Lease, Settlement, and Devise of Estates. 8vo. 1,00. Philadelphia. 1811

SUGDEN (Sir E. B.) Acts, to which are added the new Acts relating to Executors. 8vo. 2,00. London. 1830

SULLIVAN (Francis Stoughton.) Lectures on the Constitution and Laws of England, with Authorities, &c. By Gilbert Stuart, LL. D. 2 vols. 8vo. 2,50. Portland. 1825

SULLIVAN (James.) History of Land Titles in Massachusetts. 8vo. 2,25. Boston. 1801

SUMMARY of the Roman Law, taken from Dr. Taylor's Elements of the Civil Law. 8vo. 3,00. London. 1782

SUMNER (Charles.) Reports of Cases argued and determined in the Circuit Court of the United States for the First Circuit. 3 vols. 8vo. 18,00. Boston. 1836-40

These volumes contain the decisions of Mr. Justice Story on his circuit during the last three years, and form a continuation to the series of Gallison and Mason. The decisions in the present volumes relate particularly to questions of Equity and Admiralty, and are of great practical value.

SWANSTON (Clement Tudway.) Reports of Cases in Chancery, temp. Lord Endon, 1818 and 1819. 3 vols. 8vo. 13,50. New York. 1822

SWIFT (Zephaniah.) Law of Evidence. 8vo. 2,00. Hartford. 1810

SWINBURNE (Henry.) A Treatise of Testaments and Last Wills. Folio. 2,00. London. 1743

SYDNEY (Algernon.) Discourses concerning Government, to which is added Memoirs of his Life, and an Apology for Himself. Both now first published. 3d ed. 4to. 3,75. London. 1751

SYSTEM of Pleading, including a Translation of the Doctrina Placitandi. 8vo. 4,00. Dublin. 1791

SYSTEM of Stiles as now practised in the Kingdom of Scotland. 2 vols. 4to. 4,00. Edinburgh. 1774

TALBOT (Charles, Lord Chancellor.) Cases in Equity temp. Talbot. 8vo. 2,50. Dublin. 1793

TAUNTON (William Pyle.) Reports of Cases in the Common Pleas and other Courts, from Mich. Term, 48 Geo. III. 1807, to Hil. Term, 95 Geo. III. 1819, 8 vols. 8vo. 20,00. New York. 1810-23

TAYLER (Thomas.) Law Glossary. 3,50. Albany. 1833

TAYLOR (John.) Elements of the Civil Law. 4to. 6,75. Cambridge. 1755

TAYLOR (John.) Summary of the Roman Law, taken from the Elements of the Civil Law, by Dr. Ellis, &c. 8vo. 2,50. London. 1772

TAYLOR (John.) Treatise on the Law of Landlord and Tenant, with Selection of Precedents. 8vo. 3,50. New York. 1844

TAYLOR (John Louis.) Cases in the Superior Courts of Law and Equity of North Carolina, from 1816 to 1818. 8vo. 2,50. Raleigh. 1818

TERM Reports. See *Durnford and East.*

TERMES de la Ley, or Difficult and Obscure Words of the Laws explained. 8vo. 2,00. Portland. 1812

TERRIEN (Guillaume.) Commentaires du Droit Civil observé au Pays et Duché de Normandie. Folio. *cf.* 6,00. Paris. 1574

TEULET et Loiseau, Les Codes, édition pocket, tenue toujours au courant des Changements de la Législation. 18mo. 1,62. Paris. 1840

THACHER (Peter O.) Reports of Criminal Cases tried before the Municipal Court of the City of Boston, before Peter Oxenbridge Thacher, Judge of that Court, from 1823 to 1843. Edited by Horatio Woodman, of the Boston Bar. 8vo. 4,00. Boston. 1845

THEOBALD (William.) Law of Principal and Surety, and Principal and Agent, chiefly with reference to Mercantile Transactions. 8vo. 3,50. New York. 1836

THESAURUS Brevium, or Approved Forms of Writs and Pleadings to those Writs. 2d ed. Folio. 2,50. Lond. 1687

THESAURUS Juris Romanis, continens Rariora Meliorum Interpretum Opuscula cum Prefatione Ev. Ottonis. Folio. *parchment.* 5 vols. 22,50. Leyden, 1725

THOMAS (B. F.) The Town Officer, a Digest of the Laws of Massachusetts relating to the Duties, &c. of Town Officers. 12mo. 1,25. Worcester, Mass. 1845

THOMAS (J. H.) Systematic Arrangement of Coke Littleton. See *Coke.*

THURLOE (John, Secretary to Oliver Cromwell.) Collection of State Papers, containing Authentic Memorials of the English Affairs, from the Year 1638 to the Restoration of Charles II., with Life by Birch. 7 vols. Folio. *old cf.* 21,00. London. 1742

TIDD (William.) Practice of the King's Bench in Personal Actions, with References to Rules and Cases of Practice in the Common Pleas. 3d Am. from 9th Eng. ed. 2 vols. 8vo. 9,00. Philadelphia. 1840

TIDD (William.) Practical Forms; being chiefly designed as an Appendix to the Practice of King's Bench in Personal Actions. 8vo. 2,50. Albany. 1803

TOLLER (Sir Samuel.) Law of Executors and Administrators; with Additions, by Francis Whitmarsh and E. D. Ingraham. 3,50. Philadelphia. 1834

TOMLINS (Sir Thomas Edlyne.) Digested Index to the Term Reports in King's Bench, from 1785 to 1805, and in Common Pleas from 1788 to 1805. 3d ed. 8vo. 2,50. Dublin. 1806

TOMLINS (Sir Thomas Edlyne.) The Law Dictionary, defining Terms of Art, explaining the Rise, Progress, and present State of the British Law, and comprising Information on Trade and Government. 4th ed. 3 vols. 8vo. 12,00. Philadelphia. 1836

TOMLINS (H. N.) Digest of the Criminal Statute Law of England, alphabetically and analytically arranged. 8vo. 2 vols. 8,00. London. 1819

TOONE (William.) The Magistrate's Manual, being a Summary of the Powers and Duties of a Justice of the Peace, compiled from the best Authorities. 4th ed. 8vo. 5,00. London. 1828

TOTHILL (William.) Transactions of the High Court of Chancery, both by Precedent and Practice, &c. 12mo. 1,00. London. 1820

TREMAINE (John.) Pleas of the Crown in Matters Criminal and Civil, containing a large Collection of Modern Precedents. Revised by John Rice, and translated into English by Thomas Vickers. 2 vols. 8vo. 6,00. Dublin. 1793

TREVOR (Charles.) Practical Illustrations of the Laws of the Customs, with Forms and Precedents for doing Business in and out of Port, and Tables of Duties and Drawbacks. 8vo. 5,00. London. 1828

TRIALS per Pais, or the Law of England concerning Juries, &c. 8vo. 2 vols. 3,00. London. 1766

TROLLOPE (T. A.) A Treatise on the Mortgage of Ships, &c. 8vo. 2,00. London. 1823

TROPLONG (M.) Le Droit Civile Expliqué suivant l'Ordre des Articles du Code depuis et y compris le Titre de la Vente, 8vo. 15 vols. *half cf.* 47,50. Paris. 1838

TURNER (Samuel.) Practice in the High Court of Chancery. 2 vols. 8vo. 8,00. London. 1817

TYLER (Royall.) Reports of Cases in the Supreme Court of Vermont, from 1800 to 1803. 2 vols. 8vo. 5,00. New York. 1809–10

TYNG (Dudley Atkins.) See *Massachusetts Reports.*

TYRWHITT (R. P.) Reports of Cases argued and determined in the Exchequer of Pleas, and in the Exchequer Chamber in Error, in Mich. Term, 1830, to Trin. Term, 1835. 5 vols. Royal 8vo. 25,00. London. 1831–36

TYRWHITT (R. P.) and GRANGER (T. C.) Reports of Cases argued and determined in the Exchequer of Pleas, in Mich. Term, 1835, to Trin. Term, 1836. Royal 8vo. 5,00. London. 1837

UNITED STATES Digest. Digest of the Decisions of the Courts of Common Law and Admiralty in the United States.

Vol. I. By Theron Metcalf and J. C. Perkins.
" II. By George T. Curtis.
" III. By George T. Curtis.

Royal 8vo. 6,50 per vol. Boston. 1845–6

A Supplement to this work, containing a digest of upwards of 200 vols. bringing the work down to 1845, is in active preparation, and will be published in the course of 1846, and the work will then be continued by an annual supplement, after the manner of Jeremy's Annual Digest.

"WE THINK IT IS NOT EXTRAVAGANT TO SAY, THAT THIS WORK WILL BE TO THE UNITED STATES WHAT COMYNS'S DIGEST HAS BEEN, AND IS, TO ENGLAND." — *Jurist.*

UNITED STATES. Journal of the Convention which formed the Constitution. 8vo. 1,25. Boston. 1819

VALIN (R. J.) Commentaire sur l'Ordonnance de la Marine du Mois d'Août 1681, avec Notes par V. Becane. 4to. 3,00. Paris. 1828

VAN HEYTHUYSEN (F.) Essay on Marine Evidence. 8vo. 1,50. London. 1819

VATTEL (E. de.) Law of Nations; from the French. 2 vols. in 1. 4to. 2,50. *cf.* London. 1759

VATTEL (E. de.) The same. 5th Am. ed. Chitty's ed. 8vo. 3,50. Philadelphia. 1839

VENABLES (Robert.) See *Turner's Chancery Practice.*

VENTRIS (Sir Peyton.) Reports in King's Bench from 20 to 30 Car. II., and in Common Pleas, from 21 Car. II. to 3 Will. III., in 2 parts. 4th ed. Folio. 8,50. London. 1726

VERMONT Digest. See *Washburne.*

VERMONT Reports. Reports of the Supreme Court of Vermont from 1826 to 1838. 11 vols. 8vo. 44,00. St. Albans and Middlebury. 1845

VERMONT State Papers, being a Collection of Public Documents and Records, &c. &c., compiled by William Slade, Jr. 2,00. Middlebury. 1823

VERNON (Thomas.) Cases in Chancery from 1618 to 1718; by John Raithby. 2d ed. 2 vols. 8vo. 10,00. Brookfield. 1829

VERNON (T.) Cases argued and adjudged in the High Court of Chancery, originally published by Order of the Court, from the Manuscripts of T. Vernon. With References to the Proceedings in the Court, and to later Cases, together with Tables of the Names of the principal Cases, and of the Cases cited in the Notes. By J. Raithby. 3d ed., with References. In 2 vols. Royal 8vo. 7,50. London. 1828

Vernon (G. W.) and Scriven (J. B.) Irish Reports determined in the King's Courts, Dublin, with Select Cases in the House of Lords of Ireland. 8vo. 4,50. Dublin. 1790

Verplanck (G. C.) Essay on the Doctrine of Contracts. 8vo. 1,25. New York. 1825

Vesey (Francis, Jr.) Reports of Cases argued and determined in the High Court of Chancery, from the Year 1789 to 1817, with a Digested Index. By Francis Vesey, Jr. Esq. of Lincoln's Inn, Barrister at Law. In 20 vols. From the last London edition, with the Notes of Francis Vesey, Jr. Esq. and the extensive Annotations of John E. Hovenden, Esq. of Gray's Inn, Barrister at Law. The whole edited, with Notes and References to American Law, and subsequent English Decisions, by Charles Sumner and J. C. Perkins, Esqrs. 70,00. Boston. 1845

"Cambridge, Nov. 4, 1843.

"Messrs. Little and Brown:

"Gentlemen, — The Reports of Mr. Vesey, Jr., in twenty volumes, are of the highest authority, and constitute one of the standard works in Equity Jurisprudence. They contain the decisions of two of the most eminent judges that have sitten in the court of chancery, during a very considerable portion of their judicial lives; I mean Lord Eldon and Sir William Grant, whom it is impossible to name but with the highest reverence and respect for their learning and ability. A new edition, such as you propose, with references to the latest English decisions, and to those in the American courts, would greatly enhance the practical utility of the work; and the price, at which you propose to publish the volumes, is certainly very cheap, and the work will, I feel confident, receive a large patronage from the profession.

"I would recommend in an especial manner to you the propriety of republishing in the same manner the later Reports containing the decisions of Lord Eldon — such as Vesey and Beames's Reports, Merivale's Reports, Jacob and Walker, Russell, &c. &c.

"I am very truly and respectfully yours,

"Joseph Story."

"Cambridge, Oct. 25, 1843.

"Messrs. Little and Brown:

"Gentlemen, — Your proposal to reprint the Reports of Mr. Vesey, the younger, can need no commendation of mine, since they are so well known to the profession, and are so highly esteemed for their accuracy and fulness of learning, in the reported judgments of some of the greatest minds which have shed lustre, in any age, on the administration of equity. I have no doubt that the profession will liberally patronize the undertaking.

"Respectfully, your obedient servant,

"SIMON GREENLEAF."

VIDIAN (Andrew.) A Book of Entries of Choice, Select, and Special Pleadings in the Court of King's Bench, with the Method of Proceeding in all manner of Actions in the same Court. Folio. 2,00. London. 1684

VINER'S Abridgment, with Supplement. By several Gentlemen. 30 vols. 8vo. 50,00. London.

VINNIUS (Arnold.) In Quatuor Libros Institutionum Imperialium Commentarius. 3d ed. 4to. 2,25. Amsterdam. 1659

VIRGINIA Cases, chiefly relating to the Penal Laws of the Commonwealth, copied from the Records of the General Court, from 1789 to 1814, with Explanatory Notes, by Judges Brockenbrough and Holmes. 2 vols. 8vo. 9,00. Philadelphia. 1815–23

VIRGINIA Reports. By Gilmer. Vol. I. Richmond. 1821

VOET (Johannes.) Commetarius ad Pandectas. 4th ed. 3 vols. Folio. *cf.* 15,00. Brussels. 1773

WALKER (John.) See *Jacob's Chancery Cases.*

WALKER (Timothy.) Introduction to American Law. 8vo. 5,00. Philadelphia. 1837

WALLACE (J. B.) Reports of Cases in the Circuit Court of the United States for the Third Crcuit. 2d ed. 3,00. Philadelphia. 1838

WALTER (Ferdinand.) Manuel du Droit Ecclesiastique de toutes les Confessions Chretiennes. 8vo. 2,75. Paris. 1840

WAMESIUS (J.) Responsorum ad Jus Forumque Civile Pertinentium Centuria Prima. Folio. 3 vols. *Parchment.* 10,00. Antwerp. 1665

WARD (Robert.) Inquiry into the Foundation and History of the Law of Nations in Europe, from the Time of the

Greeks and Romans to the Time of Grotius. 2 vols. 8vo. 4,50. London. 1795

WARE (Ashur.) Reports of Cases argued and determined in the District Court of the United States for the District of Maine. 8vo. 4,00. Portland. 1839

WARRAND (A. K.) The New Bankrupt Court Act, with Notes, &c. 12mo. *bds.* ,62. London. 1831

WARRAND (A. K.) The same in 2 vols. London. 1708

WARREN (Samuel.) A Popular and Practical Introduction to Law Studies, and Guide to the Legal Profession in all its Branches, Civil, Criminal, and Ecclesiastical; containing Elementary Outlines of the Doctrines and Practice of each, the Duties of their respective Practitioners, and copious Directions for Professional as well as General Education. With an Appendix, containing a careful Selection of the most Characteristic Pleadings and Proceedings in each Department of Equity, Common Law, Conveyancing, and of Criminal and Ecclesiastical Pleading, with Chapters on the State of the Law in Ireland and Scotland. Designed for the Use of Students, Junior Practitioners, (whether as Counsel or Solicitors,) and the Parents and Friends of those designed for the Legal Profession. 8vo. 1100 pp. 2d ed. 3,50. London. 1845

WARREN (Samuel.) Select Extracts from Blackstone's Commentaries. 8vo. 2,25. London. 1837

WASHINGTON (Bushrod.) Reports of Cases in the Circuit Court of the United States for the Third Circuit, from 1803 to 1827, edited by Richard Peters, Jr. 4 vols. 8vo. 20,00. Philadelphia. 1826–29

WASHINGTON (Bushrod.) Reports of Cases in the Court of Appeals of Virginia, from 1790 to 1790. 2 vols. 8vo. 6,00. Richmond. 1798–9

WASHINGTON (Joseph.) Abridgment of the Statutes of William and Mary, and William III. 8vo. 1,75. London. 1699

WATKINS (C.) Principles of Conveyancing, designed for the Use of Students; with an Introduction on the Study of that Branch of the Law. 7th ed., with large Additions, containing the Law relative to the Creation and Transfer of Estates and Interest in Real and Personal Property. By Richard Preston. Royal 8vo. 1,50. London. 1829

WATKINS (C.) The same, by J. Merrifield. 8vo. 5,00. London. 1833

WATKINS (Charles.) Essay on the Law of Descents, with an Appendix on the Distribution of the Personal Effects of Intestates. 2d ed. 8vo. 2,00. Dublin. 1794

WATKINS (Charles.) Treatise on Copyholds. 3d ed. Revised and brought down by Vidal. 2 vols. 8vo. 4,50. London. 1821

WATTS (Frederick,) and SARGEANT (Henry J.) Reports adjudged in the Supreme Court of Pennsylvania. 6 vols. 8vo. Per vol. 6,00. Philadelphia. 1845

WELFORD (Richard Griffiths.) A Practical Treatise on Equity Pleadings, with Observations on the new Orders of 1841, and an Appendix containing those Orders. 8vo. 2,50. London. 1842

WENDELL (John L.) Reports of Cases in the Supreme Court, and in the Court of Errors of New York, from 1828 to 1842. 26 vols. 8vo. Per vol. 6,00. Albany. 1829–42

WENTWORTH (J.) Complete System of Pleading, comprehending the most approved Precedents and Forms of Practice. Royal 8vo. 10 vols. 15,00. London. 1797–99

WENTWORTH (Thomas.) Office and Duties of Executors. 8vo. 2,50. 14th London ed. Edited by Henry Jeremy. 1829

WENTWORTH (John.) Index to his System of Pleading. 8vo. 2,00. New York. 1822

WESKETT (John.) Digest of the Theory, Laws, and Practice of Insurance, arranged in alphabetical order. 8vo. 3,50. Dublin. 1794

WESTERN. See *De Lolme.*

WHARTON (T. J.) Digest of the Reported Cases in all the Courts of Pennsylvania, together with some Manuscript Cases. Vol. I., containing Cases published since the 15th vol. of Sergeant and Rawle. 8vo. 6,00.

WHARTON (T. J.) Reports of Cases in the Supreme Court of Pennsylvania, in the Eastern District. Vols. I. and II. Per vol. 5,50. Philadelphia. 1836

WHEATON (Henry, LL.D.) History of the Law of Nations in Europe and America, from the earliest times to the Treaty of Washington. 8vo. 6,00. New York. 1845

WHEATON (Henry.) Reports of Cases in the Supreme Court of the United States, from 1816 to 1827. 12 vols. 8vo. 48,00. New York and Philadelphia. 1816–27

WHEATON (Henry) *v.* PETERS. Report of Copyright Case, decided in the Supreme Court of the United States. 8vo. 1,00. New York. 1834

WHEATON (Henry.) Digest of the Law of Maritime Captures and Prizes. 8vo. 2,75. New York. 1815

WHEELER (J. D.) American Chancery Digest, being a digested Index of the Reported Decisions in Equity in the United States Courts and in the Courts of the several States. 2d ed. 2 vols. 8vo. 8,00. New York. 1841

WHEELER (J. D.) Reports of Criminal Cases decided at City Hall, New York. 3 vols. 12,50. New York. 1823

WHISHAW (James.) New Law Dictionary, containing a concise Exposition of the new Terms of Art, and such obsolete Words as occur in old Legal and Antiquarian Writers. 8vo. 3,50. London. 1829

WHITAKER (Richard.) Law of Lien. 8vo. 1,00. New York. 1834

WHITE (William Charles.) Compendium of the Laws of Massachusetts. 3 vols. 8vo. 5,00. Boston. 1809–10

WHITE (Joseph M.) New Collection of Laws, Charters, and Local Ordinances of the Governments of Great Britain, France, and Spain, relating to the Concessions of Land in their respective Colonies, together with the Laws of Mexico and Texas on the same Subject. 2 vols. 8vo. 10,00. Philadelphia. 1839

WICKSTEAD (J.) Attorney and Agent's Table of Costs. 8vo. 1,25. London. 1829

WICQUEFORT (Mousieur de.) L'Ambassadeur et ses Fonctions, dernière édition, Augmentée des Reflexions sur les Mémoires pour les Ambassadeurs, de la Reponse à l'Auteur, &c. 2 vols. 4to. 3,75. Colonge.

WIGHTWICK (Thomas.) Reports of Cases in the Exchequer, from Sittings after Hil. Term, 50 Geo. III. 1810, to Sittings after East. Term, 51 Geo. III. 1811. See *English Exchequer*. 8vo. London. 1819

WIGRAM (James.) Points in the Law of Discovery. 1st American, from the 2d London edition. With Notes and References to American Cases, by a Member of the Boston Bar. 1 vol. 3,00. Boston. 1842

This work contains a full examination of the Law respecting the liability of parties, their solicitors and agents, to produce papers in their possession during the progress of a cause — a question of daily occurrence, and of great practical utility.

"Cambridge, Oct. 15, 1841.

"Messrs. LITTLE and BROWN:

"Gentlemen, — Mr. Wigram's work on 'Points in the Law of Discovery' is one of the most valuable contributions to juridical literature which has appeared for several years. It is learned, acute, and discriminating, and discusses every topic with accuracy and fulness. I am, &c. JOSEPH STORY."

WIGRAM (J.) Application of Extrinsic Evidence to the Interpretation of Wills. 3d ed. 8vo. 2,75. London. 1840.

WILLES (Lord Chief Justice.) Reports of Cases in the Common Pleas, by Charles Durnford. 8vo. 3,50. Philadelphia. 1802

WILLIAMS (Edward Vaughan.) Treatise on the Law of Executors and Administrators, with Notes, and References to American Cases, by Francis J. Troubat. 2 vols. 8vo. 9,00. Philadelphia. 1841

WILLIAMS (Ephraim.) Massachusetts Reports. See *Tyng*.

WILLIAMS (Edward.) Precedents of Warrants, Convictions, and other Proceedings. 8vo. 2,50. London. 1801

WILLIAMS (Thomas Walter.) Abridgment of Cases in the Courts of Law, during the Reign of Geo. III. 5 vols. 8vo. 15,00. London. 1800

WILLIAMS (Joshua.) Principles of the Law of Real Property, intended as a First Book for the Use of Students in Conveyancing. 8vo. 5,00. London. 1845

WILLIAMS (John.) See *Saunders.*

WILLIAMS (John M.) See *Hobart.*

WILLIAMS (William Peere.) See *Peere-Williams.*

WILLIS (J. W.) Practical Treatise on the Duties and Responsibilities of Trustees. 8vo. 1,25. London. 1827

WILSON (Bird.) See *Bacon, Matthew.*

WILSON (George.) Reports of Cases in the King's Bench and the Common Pleas, from Hil. Term, 16 Geo. II. to East. Term, 14 Geo. III. 4th ed. corrected. 3 vols. 8vo. 10,00. London. 1799

WILSON (Serjeant.) On Common Recovery. 8vo. 1,50. Dublin. 1792

WILSON (J.) Treatise on Springing Uses and other Limitations by Deed, corresponding with Executory Devises, according to the Arrangement in Mr. Fearne's Essay. 8vo. 1,00. London. 1824

WILSON (J.) Reports of Cases in Chancery, commencing in the Sittings after Hilary Term, 1818. Vol. I. Parts 1, 2, and 3, and Vol. II. Part 1. Royal 8vo. 3,00. London.

WINTGENS (M. Willem.) Code de Commerce du Royaume de Hollande. 8vo. 2,25. Paris. 1839

WOOD (Thomas.) Institute of the Laws of England, or the Laws of England in their Natural Order. 10th ed. Folio. 4,00. London. 1763

WOOD (Thomas.) Another copy in fresh binding. 5,00.

WOODESON (Richard.) Systematical View of the Laws of England, as treated of in a Course of Vinerian Lectures, read at Oxford, during a Series of Years, commencing in Mich. Term, 1777. 3 vols. 8vo. 9,00. London. 1799

WOODESON (Richard.) Elements of Jurisprudence. 4to. 2,00. London. 1783

WOODMAN (Horatio.) See *Thacher.*

WOOLRYCH (H. W.) Life of the Right Hon. Edward Coke, Knight. 8vo. 1,50. London. 1826

WOOLRYCH (H. W.) Practical Treatise on the Commercial and Mercantile Law of England. 8vo. 2,50. London. 1829

WOOLRYCH (H. W.) The Law of Party Walls and Fences. 8vo. 4,00. London. 1845

WOOLRYCH (Humphrey W.) On the Law of Ways, Bridges, and Ferries, &c. From the London ed. 8vo. 2,00. Philadelphia. 1834

WRIGHT (Andrew.) Court Hand Restored, or the Student's Assistant in Reading Old Deeds, Charters, Records, &c., with 23 copperplates. 4to. 4,00. London. 1834

WRIGHT (Sir Martin.) Introduction to the Law of Tenures. 4th ed. second hand. 1,00. Dublin. 1769

WRIGHT (William.) Advice on the Study of the Law. 12mo. ,75. Baltimore. 1811

WRIGHT (John C.) Reports of Cases at Law and in Chancery, decided by the Supreme Court of Ohio during the Years 1831–1834. 8vo. 5,00. Columbus. 1835

WYNNE (Edward.) Eunomus, or Dialogues concerning the Law and Constitution of England, with an Essay on Dialogue; 5th ed. with Notes, and a Dissertation on a Course of Reading for Students, by W. M. Bythewood. 8vo. 3,50. Dublin. 1791

YATES (John V. N.) Collection of Pleadings and Practical Precedents, with Notes thereon. 8vo. 7,00. Albany. 1837

YEAR BOOKS; or Reports from 1 Edward I. to 28 Henry VIII. with Notes to Brooke's and Fitzherbert's Abridgments. 11 parts. French. Folio. *cf.* 60,00. London. 1678
A fine copy, in good condition, of the best edition.

YEATES (Jaspar.) Reports of Cases in the Supreme Court of Pennsylvania, with Select Cases at Nisi Prius and in the Circuit Courts, from 1791 to 1808. 4 vols. 8vo. 20,00. Philadelphia. 1817–19

YELVERTON (Sir Henry.) Reports in King's Bench, temp. Eliz. and Jac. I. 2d ed. By William Wylde. Folio. 2,00. London. 1674

YELVERTON (Sir Henry.) Reports of Cases in the King's Bench, temp. Eliz. and Jac. I.; 1st Am. from the 4th Eng. ed., with Notes by Theron Metcalf. 8vo. 3,50. Andover. 1820

LAW SCHOOL

OF

HARVARD UNIVERSITY.

The design of this Institution is to afford a complete course of legal education for gentlemen intending to practise in any of the United States; and a systematic course of studies in commercial jurisprudence for merchants and men of business. No public institution is given in the local or peculiar jurisprudence of any particular State; but the Library, consisting of nearly 12,900 volumes, furnishes ample means for the study of local law and practice; and the students are privately assisted in these studies, by the Professors, as occasion may require.

No particular course of previous study is requisite for admission; but every student is required to produce testimonials of his good moral character; and to give a bond of $200 to the Steward, with a surety resident in Massachusetts, conditioned for the payment of all college dues; or, instead of a bond, he may deposit $150 with the Steward, at the commencement of each term, to be retained by him till the end of the term, and then to be accounted for. No student is matriculated until such testimonials are produced and security given. The tuition fees are $50 a term, and $25 for half or any lesser fraction of a term; which entitles the student to the use of the College and Law Libraries, and Text Books, and a free admission to all the public Lectures in the University. Instruction may be had in any Foreign Language taught in the University, for the additional fee of $10 a year for each language studied. The necessary expenses of a student who resides all the year in Cambridge, will not exceed the following: Tuition $100 — rent and care of room, with use of furniture, averaging about $78 — Board from $91 to $182 — Fuel from $15 to $30 — Washing from $15 to $30. Total $299 to $420, exclusive of clothes and what is termed pocket money.

In regard to the amount of pocket money, neither expediency nor the usages of society require that it should be large.

Students who have pursued their studies in this School for three terms and Attorneys at Law who, after having been admitted to the bar in States where a previous course of study for at least one year is required, have pursued their studies in this School for two terms, are entitled, upon the certificate and recommendation of the Law Faculty, and after passing a satisfactory examination, to the degree of Bachelor of Laws.